Becoming a Commander of Covenant Wealth

D0037384

Becoming a Commander of Covenant Wealth

Dr. Leroy Thompson Sr.

Darrow, LA

Unless otherwise indicated, all Scripture quotations are taken from the *King James Version* of the Bible.

Scripture quotations marked (*Amplified*) are taken from *The Amplified Bible*. *The Amplified Bible, Old Testament* copyright © 1965, 1987 by The Zondervan Corporation. *The Amplified New Testament,* copyright © 1954, 1958, 1987 by The Lockman Foundation. Used by permission.

Becoming a Commander
of Covenant Wealth
ISBN-13: 978-1-931804-36-3
ISBN-10: 1-931804-36-2
Copyright © 2005 by Dr. Leroy Thompson Sr.
Ever Increasing Word Ministries
P.O. Box 7
Darrow, Louisiana 70725

Published by Ever Increasing Word Ministries
P.O. Box 7
Darrow, Louisiana 70725

Printed in the United States of America. All rights reserved under International Copyright Law. Contents and/or cover may not be reproduced in whole or in part in any form without the express written consent of the Publisher.

Contents

Introduction   I

1. Wealth Is the Will of God for You!   1

2. The Power and the Purpose of the Covenant   11

3. Once You've Located Yourself,
   It's Easy To Locate Covenant Wealth!   23

4. Wealth By Works—How to Bypass
   the Covenant and Forsake Your Blessing   37

5. Becoming a Steward First:
   How to Receive and Handle Wealth   43

6. Seedtime and Miracle-Multiplication Harvest   57

7. Having the Right Mindset for Miracle Money   71

8. Manifestation Secrets   77

9. Miracle Insight and Mystery Understanding   83

10. Covenant Wealth and the Prophet's Ministry   93

11. How to Receive a Prophetic Breakthrough   99

12. Becoming a Wealth-Commanding
    Money Magnet for God!   113

Introduction

For many years now, I have carried with me an assignment from God to teach believers how to prosper God's way—according to His Word and His will. I spend much time instructing the people of God concerning His will for their financial success and well-being, because many can't seem to get it through their heads that God wants them to be rich! Guilt, fear, religious teaching, and the doctrine and traditions of men have held them in doubt of their place with God and have blinded them to the truth about what Jesus came to the earth to do for them.

Jesus came to reconcile man to God, to secure eternal life and an eternal dwelling-place for us with Him, and to set captives free. Yet how many in the Body of Christ are struggling and floundering in so many areas, including financially? Their energies are being spent trying to prosper, but they are spending themselves—literally giving their lives—trying to prosper on the world's system of wealth.

God never intended that His children live that way. That's why I have remained faithful through the years to teach the Scriptures, God's holy written Word, on the subject and to share my experiences—to bring light to people's minds so that with their hearts, they can reach out and lay hold of the realities of God concerning money.

And what are the realities of God concerning money? God's reality is that if you are in Christ, you are the seed of Abraham, God has given you the power to get wealth, and He wants to establish and make known His covenant in the earth among men—*through you*! God needs believers who will rise up and show forth His blessings in the earth. God wants His children to start commanding wealth instead of crying, begging, and scraping to get by.

There are a few prerequisites to becoming a commander of wealth in the earth, and the first one is, you must know and be convinced for yourself that wealth is the will of God for you! Without that revelation in your heart, you will never progress beyond receiving a little blessing here and there while you wait for your "ship to come in" or for the Sweet By-and-By when you get to Heaven.

But, friend, the place for your prosperity is here, and the time is now. *Today* is the day of salvation! God has done it through the Person of the Lord Jesus Christ. And He has done it for *you*, not just for a select few. I am a living, breathing example of God's faithfulness to reach out to a hungry heart and to bestow revelation knowledge and divine instruction to change a life completely. God spoke to me and began teaching me when I was broke and in debt with no signs in the natural of ever coming out. But everything changed for me when I laid everything on the line before God and allowed Him to bring me out of debt and distress.

Those days of experiencing poverty and lack in abundance are only a memory to me today! But God lets me remember so I can show others the way—so that I can show you that He has no favorites, and what He has done for me, He will do for you too.

Will you partner with God in these last days to walk in your authority and command wealth on His behalf—to do with money whatever He desires and to ensure that you and family are blessed beyond your wildest imagination and dreams?

The time can come when you will move beyond living paycheck to paycheck to the point of never thinking again about whether you'll have enough. Your "more-than-enough" God—the One who is in covenant with you—can move you to a place of commanding large amounts of wealth, such as you have never seen before! You can get to the place where you can live where you want, eat where you want, wear what you want, drive what you want, and, most importantly, *sow* what you want! But it's up to you more than it's up to God whether you move into position to command wealth as a partner with Him and His work.

Though the scope of this book is a broad study to equip and prepare you to walk in divine prosperity, there are seven foundational truths you must know to become a commander of covenant wealth—in other words, to get you to the place where you're not *asking* but *commanding* wealth on the behalf of the Father. They are: (1) *the multiplication factor*, which I discuss in Chapter Six; (2) *manifestation secrets*, which can be found primarily in Chapter Eight; (3) *maintaining the flow*, which I refer to in Chapter Six; (4) *miracle insight* and (5) *mystery understanding*, which I discuss in Chapter Nine; (6) *divine moments*, also found in Chapter Nine; and (7) *mastering the ability of Jesus with wealth*, which I discuss briefly in Chapter Twelve.

As you will see throughout the pages of this book, money is not the issue in receiving divine prosperity; it is faith in knowing who you are. Instead of trying to hold on to money, we need to hold on to God's Word and never let it go. It is when you get bold, not afraid, with money that money will come to you in abundance. So read this book with a heart and mind that are open to the truth. As you do, that truth will set you completely free to enjoy your covenant of wealth.

CHAPTER ONE

Wealth Is the Will of God for You!

N ow the Lord had said unto Abram, Get thee out of thy country, and from thy kindred, and from thy father's house, unto a land that I will shew thee:

And I will make of thee a great nation, and I will bless thee, and make thy name great; and thou shalt be a blessing:

And I will bless them that bless thee, and curse him that curseth thee: and in thee shall all families of the earth be blessed.

— Genesis12:1-3

God Almighty made a covenant with Abraham, whom we have come to know as the father of faith. And that covenant included divine prosperity. It was a covenant of wealth. God desired that Abraham walk in wealth, and God desires no less for us today who are the seed of Abraham (Gal. 3:29). In Christ, we need to know that we have a covenant with God— a covenant that includes financial and material wealth.

If you are in covenant with God through the New Birth (and if you have accepted Jesus Christ as Savior, you need to know that you *are* in covenant with God), He wants you to learn how to become a commander of covenant wealth. What does that mean? It means you're not *asking*, but *commanding* wealth on behalf of the Father to use as He sees fit—for His plans and purposes. And one of His purposes for wealth is to bless His children abundantly! Wealth is a covenant promise of God to His children that comes through their faith in and their obedience to Him.

In Genesis 12:1-3, we read that after God had spoken to Abram in verse 1, commanding him to leave his country and to go to a different land, God said something else to Abram. God said that He would bless him and make him a blessing. Abram, who later was named Abraham, obeyed the Lord, and we know that God fulfilled everything He had spoken to Abraham concerning that covenant promise.

It's Not Enough To Know Your Rights—
You Have To Know Your Ability!

Let s look at another statement concerning the covenant that God made through Moses.

DEUTERONOMY 8:18

18 But thou shalt remember the Lord thy God: for it is he that giveth thee power [or ability] *to get wealth, that he may establish his covenant which he sware unto thy fathers, as it is this day.*

We can see from these verses—Genesis 12:1-3 and Deuteronomy 8:18—that not only does God want us to walk in covenant wealth, He has given us the *ability* to walk in covenant wealth.

Deuteronomy 8:18 says, *"But thou shalt remember the Lord thy God: for it is he that GIVETH THEE POWER TO GET WEALTH, that he may establish his covenant...."* God gives you the ability to walk in covenant wealth. Why? That He may establish and make firm His covenant with you.

Wealth is part of God's covenant with His children for the assignment or job that He wants them to do while they are on this earth. That means walking in the overflow, walking in abundance, walking in increase, walking as the lender and not the borrower, walking in your needs and desires being met, and walking in your dreams being fulfilled and the Father's assignment being carried out while you are on this earth.

Deuteronomy 8:18 proves out this fact. We are very familiar with this passage of Scripture in which the Lord reminded the children of Israel of how He had brought them through the wilderness to a land flowing with milk and honey, a land of "more than enough." Then He began to talk to them specifically about wealth. (I will discuss the *purpose* of the covenant in greater detail in the following chapters.)

Look at Deuteronomy 8:18 again and pay close attention to it: *"But thou shalt remember the Lord thy God: for it is he that giveth thee POWER TO GET WEALTH...."* God did not say He would give you the *wealth;* He said He would give you the *power* to get the wealth. In other words, the responsibility for your getting wealth is not on God—it's on *you!* When you activate the power to get wealth, the wealth will manifest.

It was a covenant transaction for the children of Israel to become wealthy. God had made them rich. Then He cancelled their debt. They had borrowed from the Egyptians, and their debt was cancelled in the Red Sea.

Your financial well-being is a covenant matter, because God has already taken care of it for you. The Bible says that Jesus became poor that we might become rich.

2 CORINTHIANS 8:9

9 For ye know the grace of our Lord Jesus Christ, that, though he was rich, yet for your sakes he became poor, that ye through his poverty might be rich.

Jesus became poor so that through His poverty, you might be made rich! Jesus didn't become poor so that through His poverty, you might be made poor too!

Some people get super-spiritual and say that this verse is talking about *spiritual* riches and blessings. *In Second Corinthians 8:9, Paul is talking about money!* Certainly, God has provided us with spiritual blessings; Jesus died to make us rich spiritually too. But this verse is talking about another type of rich—it's talking about money!

In the eighth and ninth chapters of Second Corinthians (and I encourage you to read those chapters), Paul is talking about money. He is not talking about being wealthy spiritually. He is talking about being financially wealthy with material gain and increase in your life so that you can be a blessing. And we know that in order to be a blessing, you must be blessed yourself.

As far as God is concerned, the wealth is already yours by virtue of the covenant. As far as He's concerned, you are already rich, you are already out of debt, and you are already financially free. What *you* need to deal with is the power—the authority, the endowment, the ability, the anointing—to get the wealth manifested. You must command the wealth to come. And that is the subject of this book. I want to help you align yourself with the covenant and position yourself through the Word and through your obedience to become a commander of covenant wealth.

God gives you the endowment, the ability, to get wealth, so *"...that he may establish his covenant which he sware unto thy fathers, as it is this day"* (Deut. 8:18). You must understand that the phrase "as it is this day" means that the power to get wealth is still in existence in this generation. That means that every child of God has the ability to walk in covenant wealth. But in order to walk in that wealth, you must know and understand that wealth is the will of God for you!

2 PETER 2:1-4

1 Simon Peter, a servant and an apostle of Jesus Christ, to them that have obtained like precious faith with us through the righteousness of God and our Saviour Jesus Christ:
2 Grace and peace be multiplied unto you through the knowledge of God, and of Jesus our Lord,
3 According as his divine power hath given unto us all things that pertain unto life and godliness, through the knowledge of him that hath called us to glory and virtue:
4 Whereby are given unto us exceeding great and precious promises: that by these ye might be partakers of the divine nature. . . .

Being a partaker of the "divine nature" means that you have supernatural abilities. Yet the Body of Christ has tried to live supernaturally everywhere else but in their finances. They have their eyes on that job of theirs too much. They have their eyes on overtime too much. It's time to declare, "Jesus, You are the Lord of my finances. I'll never be broke another day in my life, because I have a covenant with You!"

How can Jesus be Lord of your finances and you stay broke? How can Jesus be the Lord of your finances while you can't pay your bills? How can Jesus be the Lord of your finances while you live like a peasant, talking about your ship coming in one day or, "In the Sweet By-and-By..."?

The day of your financial freedom is here now! The Bible says three times in Hebrews chapter 3 that "today" is the day to believe God's Word and to begin to enter into that which He has in mind for you (vv. 7,13,15).

I tell you, I am against every debt that is oppressing the Body of Christ—every car note, every mortgage, and every bill. God said that He would make His people the lender and not the borrower, the head and not the tail. He said He would put us above, not beneath (see Deuteronomy 28:13). We have been redeemed from the curse of the Law (Gal. 3:13). Contained in that curse are poverty and lack, but we have been redeemed by the precious blood of Jesus! Therefore, every child of God has the right to be financially free. This is the will of God for *you*!

PSALM 35:27

27 Let them shout for joy, and be glad, that favour my right-eous cause: yea, let them say continually, Let the Lord be mag-nified, which hath pleasure in the prosperity of his servant.

I love this verse of Scripture! The Lord blessed me with a big, beautiful home. Let the Lord be magnified, because the family that I came from didn't cause me to have this kind of house! *God* did! And if you're a child of God, we're in the same family. We serve the same God. And He has pleasure in our prosperity!

God is your heavenly Father, and you must know that wealth is the Father's will for you. You know, most fathers are not happy when they see their children in lack. What father would be excited to see his children begging? Have you ever heard some father testify, "Thank God that two of my sons are beggars"? What about God? Do you think God is happy when His children are in lack? His children will never be beggars when they learn to walk in covenant wealth. And *your* children will never be beggars when you learn the secret to walking in this kind of wealth.

But not every Christian is going to walk in covenant wealth—although covenant wealth belongs to them. Some will refuse it in much the same way some refused the message of faith when it first began to be taught by our fathers in the Gospel in the 1950s and then again heavily in the '70s and '80s. Those ministers started teaching the word of faith, trying to get people to walk by faith, and it took these men and women a long time to even get *faith* into the Church!

Then we started teaching on healing, and for quite some time—years upon years—we had to labor to produce an understanding in the Body that healing can manifest in your life supernaturally. And then when it came to being filled with the Holy Spirit, especially in dealing with many denominational people (because we had been taught wrong), there was toil and labor in the Spirit, trying to get them to see that there is a power they could receive that would produce supernatural ability in their lives. We had to put that wrong thinking in reverse and get going in the right gear to bring the baptism of the Holy Ghost, speaking in tongues, and the gifts and manifestations of the Holy Spirit to the Body of Christ so that we could operate and function in them.

So we taught and taught. We were criticized publicly and privately. Letters were written to us, books were written about us, and certain ministers even went on television and taught against things pertaining to the Holy Ghost and against the truth.

And now we have the same thing with money. We know that it is going to take teaching after teaching and anointing after anointing to get the truth across. But we are seeing that barrier of wrong teaching, traditional thinking, and unbelief cracking. The light of the truth is shining through into men's and women's hearts, and instead of getting letters of criticism, we are getting letters testifying that people are getting out of debt—and are doing it supernaturally! In the Body of Christ, we are seeing people buying other people houses and cars and sending people around the world with the Gospel, so we know that it is working.

Yet I know that it will take a while for an understanding of covenant wealth to really break through throughout the Body, but I am not quitting. I will keep teaching the truth of God's Word concerning wealth.

Make Covenant Wealth Your Reality

Covenant wealth is a reality. Supernatural debt-cancellation is a reality. Supernatural increase is a reality. Supernatural favor from God is a reality. These are biblical truths demonstrated throughout the Bible. Let the Holy Spirit help you so you can begin to see what God wants His children to have, because the assignments that God has for us are very important, and they will require that we walk in our covenant of wealth.

We've seen in Deuteronomy 8:18 that God has given you the power to get wealth. Therefore, we know that you have the *ability* to walk and live in covenant wealth. You need to know that you have that ability. It's all right if you're not walking in your covenant of wealth at this moment, but you need to know right now that you have that ability. You have the ability for every impossible situation in your life to become possible. Everything that the devil says you can't have—that is what you *can* have! It is God who empowers you to have it!

God spoke to Abraham in Genesis chapter 12 and gave some very important information for the Body of Christ about financial freedom, wealth, and increase. He said to Abraham, in effect, "Leave your country and let Me lead you to another land. Obey Me, and I will make of you a great nation and will make your name great. I will bless you, and you will be a blessing. In fact, all the families of the earth will be blessed through you."

In Genesis 15:1, God is again speaking to Abraham: *"After these things the word of the Lord came unto Abram in a vision, saying, Fear not, Abram: I am thy shield, and THY EXCEEDING GREAT REWARD."* God continued confirming His covenant with His man Abraham, and He wants to do the same with us today.

8

Someone who studies the Greek language once gave me some insight on this scripture. He said that the phrase "thy exceeding great reward" really means *I am your exceeding, rapidly increasing money supplier*!

If you still have doubts as to your covenant of wealth that God has provided through the precious blood of Jesus, I encourage you to carefully study the Scriptures for yourself. Don't let the enemy keep you back one more day from possessing what God has provided and what He *wants* you to have. God wants you to be a covenant-wealth walker! Will you do it for Him so that you can be all the blessing you can be in this earth, as Abraham was before us? I believe you will as you really come to understand that wealth is the will of God for you!

CHAPTER TWO

The Power and the
Purpose of the Covenant

But thou shalt remember the Lord thy God: for it is he that giveth thee POWER TO GET WEALTH, that he may establish his covenant which he sware unto thy fathers, as it is this day.

—Deuteronomy 8:18

The power to get wealth must be understood, because that power is a divine enabling that comes from God. We must not only understand the power that God has given us to get wealth—the power of wealth itself must also be understood. Until you can understand the ramifications of having no bills, your pockets full of money, your needs and desires met, and your dreams fulfilled, you won't become a commander of covenant wealth. The truth that this is what God wants for you has to be a reality in your life, or you will waver back and forth between two opinions about money.

When we start talking about wealth, people always harp on this scripture: *"For the love of money is the root of all evil . . ."* (1 Timothy 6:10). (Most everybody knows that scripture, but many misquote it. They'll say, "*Money* is the root of all evil.") But the Lord told me, "The problem that I have with most of My children is not the *'love* of money,' but the *'fear* of money.'" And in my ministry, I often have to deal with the "fear of money" in the Body of Christ.

Many people don't know the difference between *materialism* and *manifestations.* If you're a tither and you love God and keep, or obey, His Word, you are a candidate to receive manifestations of wealth. And when you receive them, you should not feel fearful or ashamed. When you truly love God and the things of God, and you are excited about His plans and purposes, money will not be a hindrance to you; it will be a blessing that you will use to bless others.

Some people are afraid of money. There is a fear about having excess, surplus, or overflow. They think they should have just enough. They are afraid of too much. But we should be thankful for every need supplied, because God does meet our needs, and the Bible says that every good and perfect gift comes from Him (James 1:17).

Some people "put the breaks on," so to speak when they hear someone testify of what the Lord has done for him or her financially. But when they do, they close themselves off from understanding covenant wealth. If they don't change, they will never understand or experience the reality of going where they want to go, eating where they want to eat, buying what they want to buy, and sowing what they want to sow. You can't enter covenant wealth if somebody's house or car is going to trip you up and stop the anointing.

So don't put your breaks on, or you won't understand wealth and how some people in the Body of Christ can go where they want, eat where they want, buy what they want, and sow what they want. As I said, you cannot enter covenant wealth if somebody's nice house or car is going to stop your anointing.

Christians who think the will of God for them is "just enough" don't know God very well. God's forté is blessing us. Why? He wants to make us a blessing! (How can you be the blessing financially that God wants you to be with "just enough"?) So get rid of that attitude about money, because if you're going to operate in this world, you're going to need some money to do it!

You have to prepare yourself to become a commander of covenant wealth. You have to know from the Word what God desires for you concerning money. There are charlatans out there who call themselves ministers but who are really just in the money business. There are false prophets in the Church. But none of that annihilates our covenant of wealth—our covenant of increase and favor financially and materially—that God wants us to walk in.

The Power and the Purpose

There is power in wealth. You don't have to live in this world very long to realize the power that is behind money. And there is a power or enabling that comes from God to get wealth. But there is something else we must understand about covenant wealth, and that is the *purpose* of wealth. The understanding of these three things—the *power to get wealth*, the *power of wealth itself*, and the *purpose of wealth*—must be in place for an anointing for increase to come upon you. These three things must be in place so that Satan will not trick us concerning God's blessings. For example, we just read that the love of money is the root of all evil (1 Timothy 6:10). But nowhere in the Bible does it say that money itself is evil.

It is very important for you to understand how to prosper in the Kingdom of God. It is very important for you to understand how to enjoy true prosperity. God is not going to give you something that's going to burden you. But if you don't understand what prosperity is for, it will become a hindrance to you. As you study the

Word of God for yourself, the Spirit of God will impart the truth to you that it is all right to enjoy the goodness of God. Remember He has given us all things richly to enjoy (1 Timothy 6:17).

Along with understanding God's goodness, we must understand the criteria for entering into God's system of wealth. And one of those criteria is this: The wealth is not just for you, but for others too. Remember, God said to Abraham, "I will bless you, and I will make you a blessing so that all the families of the earth are blessed." (Gen. 12:2,3). Abraham walked in the covenant as a wealthy man, but God expanded him until all the families of the earth were blessed.

Covenant wealth is really all about Jesus, not money. It's about the work of the Kingdom, the harvesting of souls. There are a lot of assignments and visions that the Lord wants to have fulfilled. This covenant of wealth is for that purpose. In the meantime, because you are His child, you get blessed in the process!

God will never use you for an assignment and not let you enjoy the benefits of it. Once, a very wealthy woman who lives on a $30,000,000 estate visited my wife and me. While we were all riding in our Rolls Royce, this woman suddenly looked at my wife and said, "This car is just a tool for God's assignment."

She was right. I have a "wealthy" assignment. God told me to preach "Money cometh to the Body of Christ." What would I look like in an old jalopy? In other words, at some point, a word has to be confirmed, or it's not a word from God. But I know, and so do a whole lot of other people, that I received a word from Heaven. And that word is producing a bountiful harvest in my life and in the Body of Christ.

The Purpose Is the Priority

Many people misunderstand money because they fail to realize that the purpose of prosperity is to accomplish God's work on the earth. That purpose is the priority. Houses and cars are fine, but they will not go to Heaven with you. They are for you to enjoy while you're here working the works of the Kingdom. Don't let the devil hoodwink you into living like a dog down here—like you don't have a covenant. The end-time Church is called to be a prosperous Church. But don't allow yourself to become distracted, either, to the point that houses and cars are all you think about.

Why the Covenant?

What is the covenant of wealth for? In Genesis 12, when God dealt with Abram about His covenant and what He wanted him to do, first, God said, *". . . Get thee out of thy country, and from thy kindred, and from thy father's house, unto a land that I will shew thee."* And we know that obedience is a prerequisite—a commanding factor, which we will look at in the next chapter—for walking in covenant wealth. But the promise of wealth that God covenanted with Abraham about was for the purpose of Abraham's blessing and the blessing of many others.

God told Abraham, "I will *bless you*," but then He said, "I will *make you a blessing.*" Now look at the last part of verse 3: *". . .In thee shall all families of the earth be blessed."* God blesses us for a purpose; He increases us for a purpose. And when we get hold of the purpose, we can begin walking in covenant wealth.

God wants us to be wealthy. Deuteronomy 8:18 says, *"But thou shalt remember the Lord thy God: for it is he that giveth thee power to get wealth. . . ."* Why would God give us the power to get wealth if He didn't want us to have wealth? He gave us the power to get wealth that He may establish His covenant with us.

So it's not really about you. This is about God's covenant. But because you're hooked up with God's covenant, His covenant covers you; it covers your situation. He gives you the power to get wealth that He may establish His covenant in your life and in the world.

The most important thing to see in this verse is that your wealth has something to do with God establishing His covenant in the earth realm. When you stay poor or broke, it is an insult to the blood of Jesus, for the Bible says that He became poor that you might become rich (2 Cor. 8:9). Having wealth is about establishing God's covenant. Therefore, if you yield to the Spirit of God, He will turn loose a financial breakthrough in your life like you have never seen before! Why? So that He can establish His covenant. He knows that you know what to do with money. Therefore, He is blessing you and making you a blessing in the earth as He did with Abraham.

I mentioned Second Corinthians 8 and 9 previously. Let's look in-depth at verse 8 of Second Corinthians chapter 9.

2 CORINTHIANS 9:8
8 And God is able to make all grace abound toward you; that ye, always having all sufficiency in all things, may abound to every good work.

God desires that you may abound to every good work. This is what it is all about. God's covenant is covering you so that you can cover His work.

God needs pipelines; He needs distributors of His blessings financially. He needs people He can trust who will love Him and channel money where He tells them to channel it. And while they are channeling it, He says, "Let Me take care of you now."

God gave His people His word that if they would do what He told them to do, they would be wealthy people. This is a promise that God has made, and it still holds true today.

You might be thinking, *I don't want to be wealthy. I don't need all of that.* No, the Lord needs for you to have it so He can get His business carried out. Wealth and riches are *supposed* to be in your house!

> *PSALM 112:1-3*
> *1 Praise ye the Lord. Blessed is the man that feareth the Lord, that delighteth greatly in his commandments.*
> *2 His seed shall be mighty upon earth: the generation of the upright shall be blessed.*
> *3 Wealth and riches shall be in his house: and his righteousness endureth for ever.*

Wealth and riches shall be in your house if you fear, or reverence, the Lord and if you delight greatly in His Word. It is wrong to have anything else besides wealth and riches in your house. All those bills in the drawer are not supposed to be in your house! People calling you to collect debts is not supposed to be happening in your house. Your mailbox is not supposed to be full of collection notices. High blood pressure, stress, and a lot of sickness and disease come from money problems, because people are worrying about money. They're trying to make ends meet, living from paycheck to paycheck. But wealth and riches should be in their house.

Friend, I'm receiving my covenant wealth! I love God and I am rich. I was poor and I loved God. Now I'm rich and I love Him even more. I used to praise God in my small house, but now I praise God in my big house!

End-Time Kingdom Purposes— Why Every Believer Should Walk in Wealth

As I said before, the purpose of covenant wealth is not about cars and houses and lands. What is God's purpose for telling us about all this wealth in His Word and showing us people like Abraham, Isaac, Jacob, and others whom He made wealthy? He talked about Solomon's wealth. He talked about how wealthy Job was. Why did God show us all of that if He didn't want us to be a part of it. He talked about wealth and increase for a reason, for a purpose.

Let's look at Matthew 6:19-21.

MATTHEW 6:19-21
19 Lay not up for yourselves treasures upon earth, where moth and rust doth corrupt, and where thieves break through and steal:
20 But lay up for yourselves treasures in heaven, where neither moth nor rust doth corrupt, and where thieves do not break through nor steal:
21 For where your treasure is, there will your heart be also.

Jesus is saying here that when you're financing Kingdom projects—when you're sowing into a vision that He has sent into the earth realm—you're laying up treasures in Heaven. Visions and divine missions come from Heaven. When you lay treasure up for that purpose, thieves can't break through and steal it, and moths or rust can't corrupt it, because your heart is not on things, but on the vision.

We need to position ourselves to become commanders of covenant wealth so that we can not only accomplish God's vision, but so that we can break out of the world's system of wealth, which is not really wealth at all. In the world's system, people are working two jobs trying to be prosperous. Wives and mothers are working when they don't want to be working, just trying to have a few things in life. In some families, everybody in the family is working, trying to meet the family's budget. The reason all this is happening is, we have gotten off God's system. Now we're trying to get back on God's system, where the money will flow like never before.

There is absolutely, positively, nothing wrong with

being rich. God is ready to take you out of the rat race of trying to obtain finances. And I believe you are ready to go!

How will you do it? For one, your heart will be on the Kingdom, on the work of God. You will lay up treasures in Heaven by putting it into Kingdom work. And when you do, you'll have Kingdom guidance over it. You'll have Kingdom protection over it, and you'll have Kingdom promises recovered and received.

I've been talking about the purpose of the covenant, which is closely tied the purpose of the *believer*. The purpose of the believer in the earth can be found in Jesus' purpose in coming to the earth.

1 JOHN 3:8
8 . . .For this purpose the Son of God was manifested, that he might destroy the works of the devil.

We're not going to destroy the works of the devil just by prayer. All the wickedness and darkness that is happening in the world today was paid for with money. The Body of Christ was sent to destroy the works of the devil. But the devil has hoodwinked the Church for many years, and we've been "churchy," broke, and weak in fulfilling our mission. We've not taken hold of the covenant that God has put in place in the earth so that we could have the dominion that we're supposed to have. As believers, we are to overcome the devil in every situation. We are to enforce his defeat; we are to enforce the fact that Jesus destroyed his works.

Jesus said, "*...Go ye into all the world, and preach the gospel to every creature*" (Mark 16:15). Well, who is going to go? If the works of the devil are going to be destroyed, the Body of Christ will have to have their money. Millions of souls have not heard the Gospel yet. How will they hear if we don't get our money. It's breakthrough time for the Body of Christ!

John revealed to us one of the main purposes of believers walking in their authority and in their wealth: to destroy the works of the devil. But the devil only wants people to see the Rolls Royces. Then religious folks protest, "You don't need a Rolls Royce to preach the Gospel," and members within the Body of Christ start fighting with one another while the enemy runs rampant in the lives of the untold and unreached.

When you realize the purpose for your wealth—when you realize that your money has an assignment—you will not hesitate to give anything up for the Lord. You will give it freely, because you're walking in your covenant of wealth.

Let's look at one woman in the Gospel of Matthew who bestowed her wealth upon the Lord and His work.

MATTHEW 26:6-13

6 Now when Jesus was in Bethany, in the house of Simon the leper,

7 There came unto him a woman having an alabaster box of very precious ointment, and poured it on his head, as he sat at meat.

8 But when his disciples saw it, they had indignation, saying, To what purpose is this waste?

9 For this ointment might have been sold for much, and given to the poor.

10 When Jesus understood it, he said unto them, Why trouble ye the woman? for she hath wrought a good work upon me.

11 For ye have the poor always with you; but me ye have not always.

12 For in that she hath poured this ointment on my body, she did it for my burial.

13 Verily I say unto you, Wheresoever this gospel shall be preached in the whole world, there shall also this, that this woman hath done, be told for a memorial of her.

This woman with the alabaster box anointed Jesus with expensive perfume, and the disciples called it a waste because they didn't know the purpose. They called it a waste because they didn't understand money. They didn't understand that ministry and money go together. What did Jesus say? He called them on the carpet, in effect, saying, "Wherever this Gospel is preached, what this woman did today will be mentioned."

Your money must have an assignment; your money must have a mission or purpose. And God must be included. Supernatural provisions will always come when one understands his financial assignment in the work of God. Understanding the power and the purpose of the covenant, that person becomes a Kingdom commander of covenant wealth.

CHAPTER THREE

Once You've Located Yourself, It's Easy To Locate Covenant Wealth!

In Chapter One, we saw from the Scripture that we have a covenant of wealth and that God wants us to walk in our covenant. In fact, the covenant was His idea. He has given us the power to activate the covenant and to walk and live in covenant wealth. And God shows us in His Word how to do it.

But first, we need to locate ourselves. We have to find out where we're at in our attitudes and motives concerning money. Then we have to locate that wealth—the covenant wealth that He has made available to us as His children.

Commanding Factors

When I talk about being a commander of covenant wealth, I'm talking about putting yourself in a position like Abraham did so that you can be a blessing. Being a commander of covenant wealth means putting yourself in a position where all of your needs and desires are met and all your dreams come true as you carry out God's assignment, helping other people get their needs met.

In order to put yourself in this position and become a commander of covenant wealth, you must have *wisdom and understanding, willingness and obedience,* and *faithfulness,* and I will discuss these factors in this chapter.

The Wisdom and Understanding Factor

Ecclesiastes 7:10-12 says, *"Say not thou, What is the cause that the former days were better than these? for thou dost not enquire wisely concerning this. Wisdom is good with an inheritance: and by it there is profit to them that see the sun. For WISDOM IS A DEFENCE, and MONEY IS A DEFENCE: but the excellency of knowledge is, that wisdom giveth life to them that have it."*

So you can see that "wisdom is a defense" and "money is a defense." But wisdom as a defense is better than money as a defense. Why? Because the wisdom will get you the money. But if you have money without wisdom, you will lose the money you have.

God has to give you divine insight and wisdom to walk in covenant wealth. And He will do it! The entrance of God's Word will give you light, which brings wisdom and understanding about your inheritance (Ps. 119:130). In other words, your wisdom and understanding concerning the wealth of God will come through the Word of God. Whether you are studying the covenant as you read and meditate on the Scriptures, or you hear the Word on finances from the mouth of an anointed man or woman of God, that is how the wisdom and the understanding are going to come: through the Word.

The Willingness and Obedience Factor

Some people say there's no profit in serving God. But don't tell me anything about serving God without receiving any material blessings! There *is* profit in serving the Lord! Do you remember what Isaiah 1:19 says? *"If ye be willing and obedient, ye shall eat the good of the land."* Well, *The Living Bible* says, "If you will only let Me help you, if you will only obey Me, I'll make you rich." Can you stand to be rich?

"If ye be WILLING and OBEDIENT, ye shall eat the good of the land." Covenant commanders have to come to the point where they are willing to do whatever it takes to do and to fulfill God's will. Whatever God says at any moment, right where they are, they will obey it. And they will do it willingly.

This is true concerning money too. You have to be ready to do with your money whatever God says to do at any given moment, right on the spot. You can make that decision now with whatever you have today. Don't think you're going to wait until you're walking in abundance to be obedient to God in finances. Tell God to call the shots with your money and with your life *today*. He will begin to call the shots to get you out from the level where you are now and raise you to another level.

You have to become willing to do whatever God tells you to do. It's as simple as that. John 2:5 says, *"...Whatsoever he* [Jesus]*saith unto you, do it."* This verse is the essence of financial miracles. This is Jesus' first recorded miracle, and Mary told us how it happened. It happened when the disciples obeyed Jesus implicitly; they did exactly what He told them to do, and they witnessed the miraculous as a result.

If you don't understand this great truth, when God tells you to give, you won't, because you'll think it's the devil. You will do whatever the Lord says to do in other areas, but what about with your money? Whatsoever He says to you, do it. Your miracle comes when you are completely sold out to what God tells you to do.

Trust God So That He Can Trust You

Do you trust God enough with the money you have to give it away as He directs? Covenant wealth comes by trusting and by being trustworthy. Can you be trusted with money? God gives covenant wealth to those He can trust. When God finds out that He can trust you—that you are going to be willing and obedient to do whatever He anoints you or gives you an unction to do—you will become a container that can't contain all the blessings that come your way!

And you won't try to hold on to them, either, because you're willing and obedient toward God to do whatever He says to do. You have the revelation in your heart, and you know that God has said, "I will bless you, and I will make you a blessing." After He has made you a blessing, you will live on the surplus. That means you can live in the house you want to be in, because God will bring your dreams to pass. He will give you the desires of your heart. (Do you have plenty of heart's desires?)

You have to position yourself for covenant wealth by obeying God and His Word and by obeying divine instructions. Then money will come to you because God knows He has found somebody in you that He can trust. God will trust you if you trust Him.

The Body of Christ should be surrendering everything they have to God. God is looking for trustees whom He can trust with wealth so that He can call on them to disperse and distribute that wealth as He desires.

'Remember Me': A Money Test

There is another aspect of obedience that has to do with acknowledging God for your wealth once He brings you to that level.

DEUTERONOMY 8:17,18

17 And thou say in thine heart, My power and the might of mine hand hath gotten me this wealth.

18 But thou shalt REMEMBER the Lord thy God: for it is he that giveth thee power to get wealth, that he may establish his covenant which he sware unto thy fathers, as it is this day.

It is very important that you remember the Lord your God, the One who revealed the truth to you and helped you walk in it. Actually, you need to remember the Lord *before* you begin walking in covenant wealth and *afterward*. When you put yourself into this mode and mindset before covenant wealth begins happening for you, you pass the money test without money being involved.

You see, God wants to know how much you love Him. If He raises you up in the area of finances, will you remember Him? Will you testify that He did it? Or will you forget that He is the One who gave you the power to get that wealth?

A Covenant Commander Is a Commandment Keeper

There are requirements that we must meet so that God can trust us in the area of wealth—so that He can trust us to be a commander of covenant wealth, having no bills, no debt, and no money troubles. God needs to be able to trust us so that money is not a thought in our life anymore. Our trust is not in money, but in God. We are obedient to Him before He prospers us, *while* He is prospering us, and *after* He prospers us.

Read carefully the following passage that further deals with the blessings of the obedient.

DEUTERONOMY 28:8-13

8 The Lord shall command the blessing upon thee in thy storehouses, and in all that thou settest thine hand unto; and he shall bless thee in the land which the Lord thy God giveth thee.

9 The Lord shall establish thee an holy people unto himself, as he hath sworn unto thee, if thou shalt keep the commandments of the Lord thy God, and walk in his ways.

10 And all people of the earth shall see that thou art called by the name of the Lord; and they shall be afraid of thee.

11 And the Lord shall make thee plenteous in goods, in the fruit of thy body, and in the fruit of thy cattle, and in the fruit of thy ground, in the land which the Lord sware unto thy fathers to give thee.

12 The Lord shall open unto thee his good treasure, the heaven to give the rain unto thy land in his season, and to bless all the work of thine hand: and thou shalt lend unto many nations, and thou shalt not borrow.

13 And the Lord shall make thee the head, and not the tail; and thou shalt be above only, and thou shalt not be beneath; IF THAT THOU HEARKEN UNTO THE COMMANDMENTS OF THE LORD THY GOD, WHICH I COMMAND THEE THIS DAY, TO OBSERVE AND TO DO THEM.

It is very important that you keep God's commandments. You will never become a "commander of the covenant" unless you keep the commandments of God. If you want to be a *covenant commander*, you will have to be a *commandment keeper*.

We're Blessed in Our Obedience, and We're a Blessing When We're Blessed!

Now let's go back and look in greater detail at what God told Abraham in Genesis chapter 12. In this passage, God points out various aspects of becoming financially free. (One of the quickest ways to get out of debt and walk in financial freedom is to tell God that you want to be a blessing. So say to Him from your heart, "I want to be a blessing. I don't just want to be blessed. The priority in my life, Lord, is to be a blessing.")

GENESIS 12:1-3

1 Now the Lord had said unto Abram, Get thee out of thy country, and from thy kindred, and from thy father's house, unto a land that I will shew thee:

2 And I WILL MAKE OF THEE A GREAT NATION, and I WILL BLESS THEE, AND MAKE THY NAME GREAT; and THOU SHALT BE A BLESSING:

3 And I WILL BLESS THEM THAT BLESS THEE, AND CURSE THEM THAT CURSETH THEE: and IN THEE SHALL ALL FAMILIES OF THE EARTH BE BLESSED.

In this passage, before God enumerated the blessings to Abraham, God dealt with Abraham about what He wanted Abraham to do: ". . .Get thee out of thy country, and from thy kindred, and from thy father's house...." Abraham obeyed God and left.

Wouldn't *you* obey God and leave a certain place if He told you all the blessings He was going to bring upon you for doing it? I know I would. In fact, I *did* it! I quit my job because the Lord told me to do it. He told me He would take care of me, and He has done it! I am walking in covenant wealth today as a result of my obedience to God.

There are covenant promises for the obedient today. If you're not walking in your covenant of wealth, your problem might be disobedience. Your family may have a hold on you, and that might be your problem right there. God is calling you to different places, but you can't go because your favorite cousin doesn't want to go or your mama doesn't want to go. Jesus said, *"Think not that I am come to send peace on earth: I came not to send peace, but a sword"* (Matt. 10:34).

I'm telling you, you will not break out of the stagnation and frustration you're experiencing unless you become independent of everyone except Jesus Christ! You will not come out of any spiritual or financial rut you might be in unless Jesus is calling the shots in your life. You can't have all of those other people speaking into your life when the Lord is calling you out. The Bible says if you are *willing and obedient*, you shall eat the good of the land (Isa. 1:19).

If you're going to walk in covenant wealth, you will have to be controlled by God and His Spirit, not by other people and their opinions. Simply put, you might just have to cut some people loose. Now, I'm not talking about leaving a spouse behind just because he or she isn't where you are spiritually or doesn't believe exactly like you believe. I'm talking about relatives outside your immediate family, and friends or associates who might be hindering you from obeying God.

God called Abraham out from among his family, and He did the same thing with me. I have four brothers, and we all lived on one tract of land. My sister lived on another lot nearby. We had a little Ponderosa! My daddy had gotten some land, so we had all built our homes together.

Now, in my mind, I wasn't ever going to leave the "Ponderosa"! But God had other plans. He led my wife and me out into another area of town. And I am so glad we left! We have been blessed "exceeding abundantly above" (Eph. 3:20) as we have obeyed the Lord.

One rainy day, my wife and I were on our way home from church, and God led us into a certain area in Gonzales, Louisiana, to a very prestigious subdivision. I called the man who was selling the lots, and he came over to meet us. We told him that we wanted to look at some lots, so he got into our car with us to show us around.

Now, we didn't have any money. We just wanted to see some lots, because the Lord had led us there. Some houses had been built there already, so this man took us to the back of the subdivision. I said, "Sir, I have been in the back all of my life. I don't want one of these lots back here." So he showed us lots that were closer to the front.

Finally, we arrived at two particular lots, and I got out of the car and started walking around. He got out of the car, too, and before long, I looked at him and said, "I'll take them both." I didn't have any money, but the Lord had sent me there. And do you know that the Lord provided all the money we needed? We built our house, taking up both of the lots. In that particular subdivision, you can't put a fence up. But because we had two lots, that overrode the covenants and laws of that area, and it gave us the right to put up a fence. Sometimes tour buses pass my house, so I had to get a gate put up. It's one of those Buckingham Palace type of gates.

I said all that to say this: If you are obedient to God, He will call you out from lack, from want, and from living from paycheck to paycheck. My ministry is based on this fact. I was a nobody who God blessed and made a somebody. I read in the Book of Revelations that ". . .they overcame him [the devil] by the blood of the Lamb, and by the word of their testimony" (Rev. 12:11). So when I talk about these things and share them, I don't have any room to brag. I am only saying these things to let you know that since God did this for me in the Deep South, He can do something for you wherever you are!

In teaching on the subject of wealth, I always talk about this important aspect of obedience and yieldedness to the will of God, because people can misunderstand what I'm saying if I don't talk about it. They don't get the full picture. In other words, some people can get caught up with the "blessings" part of the covenant and forget the part about *being* a blessing.

Walking in covenant wealth is not just about having houses and cars and diamonds. Yes, those are all included. The Lord says to delight yourself in Him, and He will give you the desires of your heart (Ps. 37:4). Giving you your heart's desires is no big deal with God. But receiving from God is not just about *your* dream and *your* vision. And we need to know that and have it straight in our heart and mind before we can walk in covenant wealth.

The Faithfulness Factor

We know that God chose the foolish things of this world to confound the wise (1 Cor. 1:27). People all over the country want to know about me. "How is he prospering that much?" "Who is he?" "Where did he come from?" It's because God's hand is upon me. And He is no respecter of persons (Acts 10:34). What He has done for me, He will do for you too!

Nobody knew me when I was working in a sugar cane field. There were no preachers in my family. I had no religious background, and I was not reared in church. My parents never read the Bible in my presence. No one said anything about Jesus or God. But when I was in my 20s, one Sunday morning, I went to church and got born again! And I've never been back in the streets again, because I consecrated myself to the Lord.

You can have all the confessing you want, but if you don't consecrate yourself—if you don't line up with God's holiness—you won't be able to receive from God like He wants you to receive. God is looking at your faithfulness over a protracted period of time. He is looking to see if you'll walk with Him day after day, come what may, and if you'll hold on to His Word in the good times and in the bad.

You can't make a good confession and then in the same breath say, "It won't work." You'll stop the flow of God's blessings if you do that. It's just like going to the doctor because your heart isn't working right. The first thing you want him or her to do is see if there are any clogged arteries stopping the blood flow. Well, your faith needs to flow too! You read the Word and make good confessions, but it won't add up or amount to much if the faithfulness factor isn't present—if you're not being consistent with your faith.

And oftentimes, the consecration factor is missing in a believer's life. When that happens, Satan, the accuser of the brethren, says to God, "You can't let her become financially free because I've got this, this, and this on her." He tells God, "You can't violate Your own Word," and he's right: God won't go against His Word. So if *you're* going against God's Word, you shut God down where your blessing is concerned even though God wants to bless you. You and Satan can shut God down!

I know what I'm talking about concerning commanding covenant wealth. I am a product of what I'm teaching. I was a man in debt up to my grandma's neck! But light came and wisdom and understanding came; willingness and obedience and dedication came. An affection came to me for the Word of God and for the things of God, and with that affection came an addiction—a Holy Ghost addiction to doing God's will.

We have to walk in *wisdom and understanding* of the covenant, in *obedience*, with *willingness*, to the covenant, and in *faithfulness* to the covenant if we want to experience the wealth that the covenant provides.

Locating Our Covenant Wealth

The wealth that belongs to you and me as God's children—as partakers of the covenant—is not up in Heaven. Everything that we could ever want or need in the way of money is right here in the earth (Ps. 50:10; Haggai 2:8). God put it here for us. The Bible says it belongs to Him. And what belongs to Him belongs to us, His children.

I was preaching in another state one time, and my son and I were in our hotel room just relaxing one particular night. I was watching television, and a program came on that showed the homes of celebrities and others who had great wealth. One home cost $128,000,000. (What could you do with a $128,000,000 house!)

As I was watching that program, I became angry. One guy had bought an $80,000,000 home and then a $70,000,000 home somewhere else. And one movie star made the statement: "A million dollars is like a hundred dollars to me." These people are living in multi-million dollar houses, yet many of them are telling us ministers that we can't preach on prosperity!

Some of the ungodly people who have all that money wouldn't thank God or acknowledge Him for their blessings if their lives depended on it. That money should be our money! It belongs to the children of God.

PROVERBS 13:22 (Amplified)

22 A good man leaves an inheritance [of moral stability and goodness] to his children's children, and the wealth of the sinner [finds its way eventually] into the hands of the righteous, for whom it was laid up.

Proverbs 13:22 tells us that the wealth of the sinner eventually finds its way into the hands of the righteous for whom it was laid up. That means *money is on its feet headed in your direction*! I believe this is your time; this is your hour! It is the Church's time to rise up in the area of finances. Your life should be saturated with the wealth of God until it produces an overflow to others!

The world has a flow of wealth that really doesn't belong to them. Not only are you a candidate for the wealth of God as an heir of God and a joint-heir with Jesus (Gal. 4:7), but you have the ability to become a commander of covenant wealth. You have the ability to make a demand on the wealth of God.

ECCLESIASTES 2:26

26 For God giveth to a man that is good in his sight wisdom, and knowledge, and joy: but to the sinner he giveth travail, to gather and to heap up, that he may give to him that is good before God. . . .

The sinners are gathering money up and building it up and laying it up for us. And when that anointing is functioning properly in your life, all that is yours is going to break loose toward you. But you need to learn how to operate and function in that anointing.

JOB 27:16,17

16 Though he heap up silver as the dust, and prepare raiment as the clay;

17 He may prepare it, BUT THE JUST SHALL PUT IT ON, and the innocent shall divide the silver.

The just shall put it on! It is just a matter of time—just a little more teaching, a little more anointing, a little more yielding to the Holy Ghost—and we are going to "put it on"!

The wealth of the sinner is laid up for the just, and it is time for that wealth to start moving *now*! But you have to start saying, "The wealth of the sinner cometh to me now!"

You already know that it's yours, but now you are putting your mouth to it. Now you are putting your confession to it. You are becoming a commander of covenant wealth.

Just quoting a scripture is one thing, but activating the revelation of a scripture is another thing altogether. You activate the power that's in the Word when you are fully persuaded concerning that Word (Rom. 4:21).

I have plenty of money, and it all came from the covenant. I received it as a result of learning what I'm teaching you. There were lessons that I had to learn for myself and for the Body of Christ, because God has made me a gift to the Body, a sign and a wonder concerning financial miracles. I am not supposed to have what I have from a natural perspective. But I have it because of covenant wisdom and understanding, covenant willingness and obedience, and covenant faithfulness to step out and fulfill my assignment to the Body of Christ.

I am where I am by the grace and favor of God, not by anything I did in my own wisdom or strength. And you can walk in the same kind of blessing. It all starts with wisdom and understanding concerning God's Word and His will, with willingness and obedience to do whatever He tells you to do, and with faithfulness to do it no matter what.

Wealth By Works – How to Bypass the Covenant and Forsake Your Blessing

There is a lot of misunderstanding about wealth in the Body of Christ, even among ministers. Many ministers don't understand covenant wealth. They haven't grasped the truth concerning this powerful provision of our redemption.

Two Systems

Deuteronomy 8:17 and 18 points out two systems of wealth. Verse 17 points to your job, your education, and your own abilities as a means of trying to obtain wealth. Verse 18 points to walking in wealth *God's* way.

DEUTERONOMY 8:17,18

17 And thou say in thine heart, My power and the might of mine hand hath gotten me this wealth.

18 But thou shalt remember the Lord thy God: for it is he

that giveth thee power to get wealth, that he may establish his covenant which he sware unto thy fathers, as it is this day.

Let's look more closely at verse 17: *"And thou say in thine heart, My power and the might of mine hand hath gotten me this wealth."* God cannot permit this kind of attitude if you're going to walk in His covenant wealth. He cannot permit you to get on your own the kind of wealth He wants you to have, because wealth gotten on your own can destroy you. You could have an arrogant attitude about that money, boasting about how you earned it by the power of your own hand. And you could be selfish with that money. You won't do with it what God says to do with it, because you won't see it as God's money. You will see it as yours to do with as you please.

You see, if you're going to walk in covenant wealth, you'll have to know that you are just a steward handling money for God. And you have to get that principle of stewardship down pat right where you are now. You have to let God be in control of the money you have right now, before you walk in the fullness of covenant wealth. Why? Because when you get to the place where you can buy anything anywhere with cash, that money can overwhelm if you didn't get it God's way and with the attitude about money that He wants you to have.

Many in the Body of Christ are not releasing their covenant ability to walk in wealth because they are still in Deuteronomy 8:17, still trying to get it naturally.

How Covenant Wealth Doesn't Come

Covenant wealth comes not by achievement. It comes not by accomplishments. The money you make from the job you're working is seed. It's seed to sow so your wealth can grow. Contrary to what you might think, you are probably not going to pay off a house just by working. Certainly, it can be done, but that kind of mentality is a setup that could have you working the rest of your life.

If you're a covenant child trying to accomplish or achieve financial freedom by your college degree, you need to know that there is no financial freedom in college degrees. Your job or business cannot produce the wealth that God has for you.

The prosperity that God has planned for you has nothing to do with your profession, your job, or your family background. The Scriptures tell us to "hearken diligently to the voice of the Lord our God" (Deut. 11:13; 28:1). That is the qualifier: listening with the intent to *do* or *obey*. What your profession is, what color you are, and where you live or where you come from are irrelevant to covenant wealth.

First Timothy 6:17 says, *"Charge them that are rich in this world, that they be not highminded, nor trust in uncertain riches, but in the living God, who giveth us richly all things to enjoy."* The Bible says that it is God who gives us all things to enjoy. Therefore, we should obey Him and give *Him* all the credit for the wealth that is produced in our lives.

Let's look at that verse again.

1 TIMOTHY 6:17

17 Charge them that are rich in this world, that they be not highminded, nor trust in uncertain riches, but in the living God, who giveth us richly all things to enjoy.

First Timothy 6:17 tells us to be not high-minded. Some people are rich and high-minded, and some people are broke and high-minded. But God is training those of us who are in covenant relationship with Him to be humble and to recognize that it is Him, not ourselves, who gives us the power to get wealth.

The Protection of the Covenant

When you're walking in covenant wealth, you enjoy certain benefits beyond just the wealth that God places in your hands. When the anointing to prosper comes upon you, no one can curse whom God has blessed. No one can stop what God is doing in a person's life. But when you're walking in the God-kind of wealth, there will be people—even church folks—who will hate you for no reason, just because the covenant has opened up to you. They will be upset saying, "I don't know why she has to have all that." But you will be immune to their criticism, because along with that anointing that's on you, they can't curse you.

But you have to dot your "i's" and cross your "t's" in this area, because Satan will try to trip you up. If you mess around and happen to get some wealth, but you're not ready for it, you're going to be in trouble. You'll become arrogant, and some arrogant people go broke in their high-mindedness.

Let's read the first part of First Timothy 6:17 again: *"Charge them that are rich in this world...."* Where are you going to be rich? *In this world.* But if you're broke and start acting high-minded just because you got a Lexus, you *know* what you would do if you had money in your pocket and your house was paid for! So you have to get rid of that high-mindedness now. Thank God for your education and your blessings, but don't act arrogant because of them or because of anything that you possess.

First Timothy 6:17 says that God gives us richly all things to enjoy. So you can see that God wants you to enjoy yourself. The devil doesn't want you to walk in this revelation. He doesn't want God's Name associated with the enjoyment of wealth. Instead, the world has trained Christians to believe that there's something wrong with having wealth and with enjoying life. But God likes good things. I like good things too! How about you? Do you like good things? Or are you too spiritual? That may be why some people are broke; they are too "holy" for God to use them in the area of covenant wealth.

Alignment With the Covenant, Encounters in the Word

The key to your prosperity is very simple: Your covenant alignment is the issue. When you are aligned with the covenant, it means you will have what God says you can have—what He says belongs to you—and you will align yourself spirit, soul, and body with whatever He says to you.

This covenant kind of wealth blows away lawyers, doctors, and corporate CEOs. The covenant outdoes any natural profession. And God's Word is your access into this world of wealth—not your job and not your overtime. An encounter in the Word is what makes you a commander in the realm of wealth.

What is an encounter in the Word? When you truly have an encounter in the Word, you will put the Word first in your life (John 14:21-23; John 15:7). You honor God's holy Word, and it hooks you right in to the Father, to Jesus, to the Holy Spirit, and to all the provisions of God.

Psalm 119:105 further reveals the route to prosperity: *"Thy word is a lamp unto my feet, and a light unto my path."* There is no such thing as luck in the Kingdom of God. It's *light* that makes the difference between a poor Christian and a wealthy one.

You can declare, "This is my hour of prosperity, and I know that the way to receive it is through the Word of God. I am set for encounters in the Word of God. I am not going to live my life as a beggar. I'm going to be a blessing to my generation. Lord, I'm ready. I'm not looking to anyone else, not even to myself. I'm looking to You. Help me, Lord, in Jesus' Name."

As you make this declaration, the mighty hand of God will pick you up and make a mighty man or woman of God out of you! And it shall be for the glory of the precious Name of Jesus. As you make your declaration of faith, this day, the anointing to command wealth will come to your house! And with it, you're going to command yourself out of any type of struggle or test that may be coming against you, because the anointing to prosper you will be upon you!

Becoming a Steward First: How to Receive and Handle Wealth

When we talk about covenant wealth, it should be understood automatically that we're at the same time talking about stewardship with wealth. Your covenant wealth belongs to God. God gives it to you, but He is in control of what you do with it. You must always remember that you are not in control of covenant wealth.

Also, when we talk about covenant wealth, we're not talking about just a little bit of wealth. Covenant wealth bespeaks abundance—so much supply that you need to give wealth away. And you need to be totally submitted to God with that wealth. Wealth will put you in a dilemma if God is not in control.

Supernatural Money for Supernatural Assignments

To walk in covenant wealth, you must fully understand that you are only a steward of money for God. And you must fulfill this requirement of stewardship before you will be released to walk in covenant wealth. You must see supernatural increase as money that is released to you for a supernatural assignment. And you must totally submit to divine guidance in your giving—in your fulfilling of your assignments. Developing your heart as a steward or a trustee for God and His work will put you in a position to be trusted to distribute monies for Kingdom affairs. Notice for whom you are to be a steward: God. And what is the purpose? *His* work. You see, you are not in control of covenant wealth money. *God* is in control; you are just a steward. You can't get away from that fact.

Let's look at the following passages to determine how to qualify as a steward and a commander of covenant wealth.

MATTHEW 25:14,15,24-29

14 For the kingdom of heaven is as a man travelling into a far country, who called his own servants, and delivered unto them his goods.

15 And unto one he gave five talents, to another two, and to another one; to every man according to his several ability; and straightway took his journey....

24 Then he which had received the one talent came and said, Lord, I knew thee that thou art an hard man, reaping where thou hast not sown....

25 And I was afraid, and went and hid thy talent in the earth: lo, there thou hast that is thine.

26 His lord answered and said unto him, Thou wicked and slothful servant....

27 Thou oughtest...to have put my money to the exchangers, and then at my coming I should have received mine own with usury.

28 Take therefore the talent from him, and give it unto him which hath ten talents.

29 For unto every one that hath shall be given, and he shall have abundance: but from him that hath not shall be taken away even that which he hath.

In Matthew 25, we read a parable about a man who gave five talents to one of his servants, two talents to another, and one talent to another, every man according to his ability—meaning he gave it according to how much they could handle. The first two servants sowed their money and increased it. But we can see that the servant with the one talent could not handle it. He did not pass the money test; therefore, he did not qualify as a commander of covenant wealth.

Stewardship means that I am a manager for somebody else. If I am a steward of something, I am managing for somebody else whatever it is I'm the steward over. As a commander of covenant wealth and a steward of covenant money under God, I don't really own the money that comes to me. My money doesn't really belong to me. My house doesn't belong to me. Even though there is no mortgage on it, it doesn't really belong to me. It belongs to God, and He gets all the glory. (I have the lights on every night shining on those "Buckingham Palace" gates with the gold tips on top. I want everyone who passes to know that a child of the King lives in that house!)

God is big on stewardship. He calls that to our attention in Deuteronomy 8:17: *"And thou say in thine heart, My power and the might of mine hand hath gotten me this wealth."* And then the Bible goes on to say, *"But thou shalt remember the Lord thy God: for it is he that giveth thee power to get wealth, that he may establish his covenant which he sware unto thy fathers, as it is this day"* (v. 18). In the last chapter, I pointed out two systems of wealth in Deuteronomy 8:17 and 18—one system speaks of your education, career, and abilities as a means of trying to obtain covenant wealth; the other speaks of the way to actually obtain that kind of wealth. Covenant wealth comes not by natural achievement or accomplishment but by your positioning yourself to obtain it, and one way you do that is through stewardship.

God will not permit a person with a "look-at-me-and-what-*I've*-done" kind of attitude to walk in covenant wealth. A person with this kind of attitude will not see himself as a steward, handling money for God and for the Kingdom. He will see his wealth as belonging to him only, not to God.

As is said, to be a commander of covenant wealth, you have to know that you are just a steward handling money for God. And you have to get that principle of stewardship straight right where you are now in life. You have to let God be in charge of your giving today.

LUKE 6:38

38 Give, and it shall be given unto you; good measure, pressed down, and shaken together, and running over, shall men give into your bosom. For with the same measure that ye mete withal it shall be measured to you again.

I want to look at one word from this scripture, the word "measure." Your measure of giving has to be directed by the Holy Ghost. You will have to give up control of your own measure for giving, because the Holy Ghost has in mind what He's going to do. And He wants to use you to do it if you will let Him.

Remember in the Gospels the lad with the two fish and five loaves of bread? That lad had to give up his lunch. He gave it all. But who do you think those 12 baskets full of leftovers went to? In other words, that boy's measure of giving determined his measure of return.

Some people don't understand it when I challenge people during an offering. If someone puts a dollar in an offering, and I ask, "Is that all you've got?" I'm challenging him for his benefit, not for mine or for the church or ministry for which I'm ministering. Why? Because your measure determines your harvest—what you will receive. The measure with which you give will determine the measure with which you receive. In other words, your measure of giving makes certain decisions for you.

That's why I always encourage people to ask the Holy Ghost to help them work on their measure. You need to get bold enough to give $1,000! Pull out of your account some of that money you've been holding on to and put it into the right soil. *Just give it!* And do it with a boldness about you—not just boldness to *shout*, but boldness to *give*!

Do something out of the ordinary in the way of an offering. Do something to make yourself sweat! Do something that makes you feel like you want to fall on the floor when you get home! Provoke God to manifest in your life. Challenge your finances. Tell them they cannot stay the same. Say, "You are not going to run me anymore. I will run *you*!"

God will move you beyond one- and five-dollar giving. Sometimes you may have to give to the point you sweat, because it is the giving that activates and produces the receiving. You can actually sow your way out of any financial mess you may be facing!

Matthew 11:12 says, *"And from the days of John the Baptist until now the kingdom of heaven suffereth violence, and the violent take it by force."* You see, the measure to which you permit the Holy Ghost to direct you in your giving is the measure of force you put into the Kingdom that the devil can't stop.

In Chapter Three, I talked briefly about faithfulness as a factor in your becoming a commander of covenant wealth. We also saw that in obeying God, you have to trust Him enough with money that He is able to trust *you* with money. With the following passage, we're going to continue our study of faithfulness and obedience as it pertains to stewardship and walking in covenant wealth.

LUKE 16:10-13

10 He that is faithful in that which is least is faithful also in much: and he that is unjust in the least is unjust also in much.

11 If therefore ye have not been faithful in the unrighteous mammon, who will commit to your trust the true riches?

12 And if ye have not been faithful in that which is another man's, who shall give you that which is your own?

13 No servant can serve two masters: for either he will hate the one, and love the other; or else he will hold to the one, and despise the other. Ye cannot serve God and mammon.

I want you to underline the words in your Bible, *"If therefore ye have not been faithful in the unrighteous mammon, who will commit to your trust the true riches?"* (v. 11). You see, you must get to a point where God trusts you so much that He can commit His covenant wealth to your trust.

When your money becomes God's money and you are submitted to God, that money becomes righteous money. In fact, obeying this passage of Scripture will cause four things to happen to your finances: (1) It will turn unrighteous money into righteous money; (2) it will turn untrue riches into true riches; (3) it will turn money without God's hand of blessing on it to money with God's hand upon it; and (4) it will usher in the anointing to prosper!

The passages we read in Matthew 25 and Luke 16 are talking about stewardship. The principle is simple: If you are faithful over a little money, God will make you ruler over covenant money. But if you are not faithful over that which belongs to Him, He can't trust you with real money—with large amounts of wealth. If you're not faithful over unrighteous mammon, He can't bestow true riches.

To Be Faithful in Giving,
You Must First Be Faithful in the Tithe

If you haven't been faithful in the past, be faithful now toward the things of God with your money. Be faithful toward the house of God with the things you have now. But in order to be faithful with your offerings, you have to be faithful in the tithe.

When you tithe, you are setting apart money for God that belongs to Him, anyway. You are making it hallowed and holy and clean so that your offerings (money given beyond your tithes) can be considered a real seed, a pure seed, that will cause a harvest to be reaped in your life every time. In a manner of speaking, paying your tithes—the first 10 percent of your increase—is circumcising your money! You're setting your money apart for God so that His blessings will be reaped on your tithing and your giving. So every time you receive anything, take God's money out before it gets cursed, and give God His 10 percent immediately (see Malachi 3:7-12).

'Impossible Money'

As I said, your stewardship prepares you for handling supernatural money for supernatural assignments. I remember the Lord once said to me, "The Church cannot do what I want it to do with '*possible* money.' I am going to enable the Church to operate in 'impossible money.'"

Impossible money is supernatural money. Supernatural money is money that a job can't bring. Supernatural money can pay your bills *and* take care of your dreams and desires. You see, when you become a child of God, your roots are supernatural. The supernatural was designed by God to cover every area in your life, not just to take you to Heaven.

Anybody can have *possible* money. But when you start walking in *impossible* money, God is dealing with your finances supernaturally, and you can't explain it. You don't have any natural explanation to tell how you got it—how everything got paid for—and how you can do all the things you're doing for others.

"Well, how do I receive some of that impossible money?" you might ask. By proving yourself to God. By becoming someone who is faithful in his giving and in the way he's living, and who is obedient to do what God wants in every situation. A covenant commander of wealth is willing and obedient to God and His Word, and he is sold out and is faithful to do whatsoever the Lord tells him to do.

I alluded briefly to the account of Jesus' using the little boy's lunch to feed the 5,000. You see, when you're willing to give to God, He is able to give to you abundantly. He might use you to cause a need to be met, but when He does, look out for a harvest full of leftovers, or overflow blessings, coming your way!

We get so caught up in *how* God is going to do it—how He is going to bless us. But God already knows just how He is going to get *impossible* money into your hands.

JOHN 6:5,6

5 When Jesus then lifted up his eyes, and saw a great company come unto him, he saith unto Philip, Whence shall we buy bread, that these may eat?

6 And this he said to prove him: FOR HE HIMSELF KNEW WHAT HE WOULD DO.

In John 6:5, we see Jesus being followed by a multitude. He looked out on them and saw that they needed help. So He asked the disciples, "What are we going to do? How are we going to feed them?" And they began to make human excuses, such as, "We don't have enough." They didn't have enough understanding to draw on the Source—on the resources of Heaven that were available to them. They were thinking about what *they* could do. And, of course, they came up short.

That is why some people haven't gotten out of debt—they're still thinking about what they can do. They might be thinking, *Well, I can work, my wife can work, and my boy* [or girl] *can get a part-time job. Then I think we can make it.*

Away with that! You need to do away with that kind of thinking! You need supernatural help, not another job! And in the Name of Jesus, the Name above all names, supernatural help can come to your finances today, which will produce *impossible* money to your trust.

Jesus often asks you things, knowing that you don't have the answer, just so He can give you the answer! He will let you fumble around sometimes saying, "This scripture might work here, or that scripture might work." But nothing happens.

The Lord already knows how He is going to get you out of whatever problem or circumstance you may be facing today. He already knows how He's going to get you out of debt and make you rich. And He already knows how He's going to make you the envy of those around you. (You can't help being envied *and* persecuted when you're walking in covenant wealth. It comes with the territory.)

The Giving Anointing and
the Anointing to Prosper

There is a giving anointing, and that giving anointing ushers in the anointing to prosper. The way God wants you to give, you will not be able to pray about it. You need to be ready to give when God speaks. For example, I was ministering in a meeting once, talking about covenant wealth, when the anointing came just as Paul said in First Corinthians 2:4: *"And my speech and my preaching was not with enticing words of man's wisdom, but in demonstration of the Spirit and of power."* A man just stood up under the anointing and said, "I will pay off someone's house right now!"

We asked who knew how much they owed, exactly, to the penny. Most people don't know. They're just paying notes. They have 30-year mortgages, but if they just understood the truth, they wouldn't have to pay for 30 years. I paid off a 30-year mortgage off in three years!

Three women in that congregation jumped up who knew what they owed on their houses, and three men in that meeting, including the one who stood up at first, paid off their houses. One man said, "I'll take that one," another man said, "I'll take that one," and since the meeting was at my church, I said, "Wait a minute. I'll take the next one." Their mortgages were paid in full that day!

The Lord has done great things! Think about that! You leave your home with a house note and return shouting because it has been paid off! And you left for *church*, not for the *casino*! (We can't let the casino take our covenant's place.)

When the anointing to give comes upon you, you will have to have an unction to give mixed with joy—not of necessity, not grudgingly, but with an unction. You might be so busy giving, you won't even know where you are sometimes! It is an anointing to give that ushers in the anointing to prosper.

No Fear

But you can't be fearful that if you give, your rent is not going to be paid. God is not a man that He should lie. If He said it, He will make it good. (See Numbers 23:19.) Fear has to leave you. And the understanding of God's Word will cause it to leave.

You can't become rich when you're in fear. Why? Because if you do, that money will destroy you. You will become anxiety-ridden. You will constantly be thinking about that money, fearful that it's going to leave you. And guess what? With that attitude, it *will* leave you.

You have to know that if money leaves, it can come again. As a commander of covenant wealth, you have tapped into the Source, and you are not worried about it. You are not full of worry and anxiety.

You must maintain that God is your Source, not your job and not what news commentators say on television. Famine and drought have nothing to do with a commander of covenant wealth. God told Abraham to go; he did, and he went into a land where there was a famine. But in the next chapter, we read that Abraham became rich (see Genesis 12 and 13)!

God had said to Abraham: "I'll make you a blessing, and in you, all the families of the earth will be blessed." You see, you have to be a "blesser" in order to flow in God's blessing. You can't become rich with covenant wealth until you learn to flow in the anointing of giving and receiving— until you learn the principles of stewardship.

The New Testament Church should be surrendering everything they have to God. You need to know that God will trust you if you will trust Him. You also need to know that when you don't try to hold on to money, money will come to you.

You see, money is not the issue; it is faith in knowing who you are. Being a commander of wealth reaches far beyond money. Many people say, "If I only had money, I'd be all right." No. This is about more than money. A commander of wealth is above money. A commander of wealth is not just in charge of money, but of anything that comes into his life. Circumstances don't reign over him; he reigns over circumstances (see Romans 5:17).

In the Book of Genesis, we can read that Joseph became a commander-in-chief because he refused to be overcome by his circumstances. God promoted him, and the people came to Joseph and said, "Our money has failed. Can you help us?" And Joseph could help them, because he had become a commander of wealth. Joseph was in charge. He was in charge of the country's food supply.

A commander of covenant wealth becomes a distribution center for God. He distributes money as God directs. He becomes a channel or a pipeline of financial blessing.

Becoming a commander of covenant wealth doesn't always start with your having money. You have to be a steward of money wherever you are right now. Where the Bible talks about the love of money in First Timothy 6:10, it is not necessarily referring to what a person has. It is also referring to what a person *doesn't* have. You see, your giving locates you and reveals whether or not you are trusting God. For example, a person might not have anything, but is he trusting in that?

When your circumstances tell you you're broke, if you don't have a revelation of covenant wealth in your heart, you are trusting in the fact that you don't have money. That's where your faith is, and it governs your actions and behavior. You don't want to break loose with your giving to get your "receiving" working properly, because you are trusting in the $80 you have to see you through the next month.

But if that's what you're doing now, what are you going to do with $80,000? You won't be a blessing. Instead, you'll say, "But look at what I've got. I've only got eighty thousand. I'd better hold on to it in case I need it for something." You are trusting in the fact that you might not have enough. That's what you believe—that you might not have a full supply when you need it—so you hold on tight to what money you have.

But we who understand stewardship know better. We're singing a different tune about money. We know that God's unlimited resources are ours as we partner with Him in our handling of finances. As commanders of covenant wealth, we are stewards of supernatural money—*impossible* money—for supernatural assignments in the Body of Christ.

Seedtime and Miracle-Multiplication Harvest

In the last chapter, we looked at how we must handle the money we receive in order to become a commander of covenant wealth. As stewards of God's money, we must be bold in our giving. We must learn how to make a demand on the promises of God concerning wealth. We must learn to tap into the Word and the anointing that's on that Word. God *has* promised that He would cause His people to walk in wealth. Well, are you His? If you are, you need to learn how to command wealth. When you become a commander of covenant wealth, you cause wealth to obey you. You can talk to debt and have it leave you, because manifestations of God's promise and power will take place in your life.

I realize that there is a process. I know that you need patience (steadfastness and perseverance) so that after you have done the will of God, you might receive the promise (Heb. 10:36). I know all of that, but I'm telling you, one day in your life, things will change. It will happen overnight.

In my own life, I woke up one morning, and it was all over for me. In other words, all of my struggles with money were over and done with. Now I will never have another financial problem a day in my life. I will never see something I can't afford. I will never hear about a place that I can't afford to go. In my life, money is not an issue anymore. I can talk to God about other things.

I don't know exactly when it happened—I just know that it happened. But one morning, I realized it. I woke up and my wife said to me, "We could just go ahead and pay for this house, you know, and do a whole lot more besides that. Do you know how much money we have?"

I said, "What!" I really don't know how it happened in the natural. I just sowed and kept sowing. I was so happy when my wife said that to me. But I was happy before that too. I was happy to be a steward of the finances God had given me; I was happy to give. I was happy before, during, and after God made me wealthy!

There will be one seed that you will plant that will be the "fiery" seed, and God will say, "That is enough." You must be diligent in your sowing, because you do not know which seed is going to fire up your financial flow and change your life. Just know this: Your seed sown in faith begins the germination process of your financial blessing, but your continual sowing *maintains* the flow of prosperity and finances in your life.

The Multiplication Factor

Nothing happens in the Kingdom of God without seed. It is a principle; it is a spiritual law that God has set up.

2 CORINTHIANS 9:10

Now he that ministereth seed to the sower both minister bread for your food, and MULTIPLY YOUR SEED SOWN and increase the fruits of your righteousness.

One of the things that I always share with the Body of Christ is what has happened to me with the scriptures on sowing and harvesting. I have learned that God never asks you to give or sow something without the intention of giving you more.

Every time God asks you to do something, He is trying to move you to another level. That's why you have to come to a point where you trust Him completely.

Are you ready for the next level? When God tells you to give, you're not to tell Him that you have a house note, a car note, bills that are due, and so forth. No, when God speaks to you, you are to get in line properly and trust Him totally. If He tells you to do something, just do what He tells you to do, because He is about to make another move in your life.

Psalm 75 says promotion doesn't come from the east or west or south, but from the Lord. When the Lord gets ready to promote you or multiply things in your life, you have to pass certain tests. He gives you certain tests in the very area where you are to be promoted, and you are to pass those tests. And as you pass those tests, you go to another grade or level.

We saw in Second Corinthians 9:10 that the Lord gives you the seed, and I also want to point out here that He tells you where to sow the seed. Then the Lord who gave you the seed and told you where to sow it turns around and multiplies the seed He gave you to sow.

Everything we have comes from God. Whatever you have came from God. And when you make up your mind to give God full control of everything you have—watch out, because He likes that kind of action! When He finds out that He can trust you, He will trust you with more and more.

We know many scriptures, but quoting scriptures is not the only thing we need to do. We need to see the hand of God in action. Are you ready for your breakthrough? We have given "tons" of tithes and offerings. We should be having more wealthy people in the Body of Christ.

Giving With Thanksgiving

God gives you a seed to sow. He tells you where to sow it, and He sets up the soil for you. You sow that seed where God tells you to sow it, and God multiplies the seed. Then you give thanks for what God has done for you, and that thanksgiving brings on the multiplication.

Let's look at a verse in Deuteronomy 28 that tells one reason why God's people were walking in curses rather than the blessings, because the same truth applies to us today.

DEUTERONOMY 28:47

47 Because thou servedst not the Lord thy God with joyfulness, and with gladness of heart, for the abundance of all things.

There is a valuable lesson we can learn from this verse. We are supposed to praise the Lord for the abundance of all things! Say that every day. During the day, you need to praise the Lord. When you are driving to work or wherever you're going, you need to say, "Praise the Lord for the abundance of all things!" When you're driving home, praise Him for the abundance of all things. Keep that on your lips continually and watch what happens! Abundance is going to break loose in every area of your life.

But you need to do it with joy. Act like you're rich. Dance like you're rich. You have to shout like you're rich before you are. Your confession will lead to a manifestation when you get excited about what you're saying.

I have come to the spiritual conclusion that being thankful is one of the keys that causes God to bring forth multiplication in our lives. I found out that when you're thankful to God for what you have now, it will cause God to begin to multiply what you have because of your thankfulness.

In John chapter 6 when Jesus didn't have enough food with those five loaves of bread and two fish, He said, "Thank You!"

JOHN 6:8-14

8 One of his disciples, Andrew, Simon Peter's brother, saith unto him [Jesus],

9 There is a lad here, which hath five barley loaves, and two small fishes: but what are they among so many?

10 And Jesus said, Make the men sit down. Now there was much grass in the place. So the men sat down, in number about five thousand.

11 And Jesus took the loaves; AND WHEN HE HAD GIVEN THANKS, he distributed to the disciples, and the disciples to them that were set down; and likewise of the fishes as much as they would.

12 When they were filled, he said unto his disciples, Gather up the fragments that remain, that nothing be lost.

13 Therefore they gathered them together, and filled twelve baskets with the fragments of the five barley loaves, which remained over and above unto them that had eaten.

14 Then those men, when they had seen the miracle that Jesus did, said, This is of a truth that prophet that should come into the world.

After Jesus gave thanks, God fed more than 5,000 people with five loaves of bread and two fish—and then He provided 12 baskets of leftovers! Friend, there is no shortage in the Kingdom. We are not to depend on this economy to determine how much wealth we can have. We are covenant children of a covenant-making and covenant-keeping God!

A key to multiplication is being thankful for what you have now. When you begin thanking God now, it ignites the power of God on your behalf for things to start multiplying in your life. What did Jesus do with the bread and the fish? The same thing He did at Lazarus' grave: He gave thanks to God (John 11:41). Thanksgiving not only multiplies things, it releases miracle-working power on your behalf. So be thankful for what you do have, and more shall be multiplied to you.

When placed in the hands of the Master, those five loaves were no longer five loaves, and those two fish were no longer two fish. In Jesus' hands, their potential and possibility became limitless.

You see, when the supernatural kicks in, the natural must bow. And when you learn the secret of giving with thanksgiving, you enter into the realm of supernatural money where two plus two is no longer four in your life. You break into another realm as you sow your seed. If Jesus is the Lord of your finances, your money doesn't add up anymore; you will not count normally anymore. Money will finally come in so fast that you can't count it! You will have to take a rest. You'll get tired of counting money! You will come to a point where you don't know how much you have—you just know that you have more than enough. Your cup is running over! God will show His hand in your finances in a divine manner—so fast that you will not have time to comprehend it, just to accept it.

Did you know that you are never broke if you have a seed? *Never underestimate the power of a seed* [1] because Second Corinthians 9:10 said that God gives seed to the sower. (If you're broke, you might not be sowing like God wants you to sow; that might be your problem.)

When you sow your seed and keep sowing your seed, God is saying, "That's enough. My children have gone through enough. I don't care how much or how little they have. They're sowing their seed. I am going to bring them out with what they have."

When you sow with thanksgiving, Jesus is saying to you, "Quit fighting. Quit working all day and all night to get out of debt. Go home and hug your wife. Turn it over to Me; I will get you out. Quit working all that overtime and take your children on a picnic"!

'Make 'Em Sit Down!'

I want you to notice something else about the miracle in John chapter 6. In verse 10, it says there were about 5,000 men. That figure doesn't include the women and children who were there. There could have been 15 or 20 thousand people there that day who needed to be fed!

Now, here's another nugget concerning this verse. Jesus said, "...*Make the men sit down....*" I read that phrase once, and I saw that the Lord can make all your bills "sit down," because they're going to be paid supernaturally—with *impossible* money—with *two-plus-two-no-longer-equals-four* money! You will have a supernatural transaction manifested by the Holy Ghost! All of your financial handicaps and struggles will end. Don't be concerned about how it's going to happen. Just take it from the Word of God and from the man of God.

Listen, friend, Jesus Christ is the same yesterday, today, and forever (Heb. 13:8). Since He could sit 15 thousand people down and feed them from five loaves of bread and two fish, He can certainly do something for *you*!

John 6:11 goes on to say that Jesus took the loaves, prayed a prayer of thanks for them, and then gave the loaves to the disciples to pass them out to the people. When Jesus took the loaves, they were no longer five, because all the limits had been taken off. And I see all limits being taken off people today as they yield to Jesus what they have. I see the anointing to prosper coming upon them.

Jesus was not filled with stress. He knew who He was, and He knew that He lived in the realm of the supernatural. Jesus can take your bills, and all the limits can be taken off your life now. Supernatural, *impossible* money can come to your house!

Jesus Will Take You to the Next Level

Let's look again at verse 11 of John chapter 6 at what happened after Jesus multiplied the seed of that boy's lunch.

JOHN 6:11

11 And Jesus took the loaves; and when he had given thanks, he distributed to the disciples, and the disciples to them that were set down; and likewise of the fishes AS MUCH AS THEY WOULD.

"As much as they would" describes a certain level. But you can go past the level of "as much as you would," or "as much as your heart desires," to the level of "your biggest dreams fulfilled."

How big can you dream? What is it that you want? How much did it cost the last time you looked at it?

I reached the level at one point where I had as much as my heart desired. I thought I had arrived, but Jesus told me, "That is just a peek at what I can do. Let Me take you further. Let me take you to a zone of no limits." And He is truly causing my biggest dreams to be fulfilled.

Jesus said something else to me right behind that. He

said, "But you can't be afraid. The fear of what other people think has to be broken." Never be embarrassed about your blessing. It is the Lord who gave it to you. Never be ashamed of that.

You Have To See It Before You Can Have It

"If you see it, you can have a double portion." That is what Elijah said to Elisha (2 Kings 2:10). When you see the revelation of covenant wealth from the Word of God and from the man of God when he teaches it, you will receive the anointing to prosper, and your penny-counting days will be over. When you are operating in the realm of revelation knowledge—when two plus two doesn't equal four in your life anymore—the day will come when you will have more hundreds than ones in your wallet or bill-fold!

My friend Creflo Dollar has a very large ministry. Over a period of time, he kept sending for me to preach, and he would always pick me up in a Rolls Royce. He kept doing that, and, after the third time, I finally said to the Lord, "What are You saying, Lord?" For years, I hadn't realized that the Lord had done that on purpose. He was trying to tell me that you can't *have* it unless you *see* it.

Are you up to the level of "as much as you would"? What can you see yourself doing and having?

Accounts With God

Many Christians quote the following verse concerning prosperity. But you cannot claim 4:19 without the surrounding verses in context.

PHILIPPIANS 4:19

19 But my God shall supply all your need according to his riches in glory by Christ Jesus.

Before Paul wrote Philippians 4:19, he wrote the following.

PHILIPPIANS 4:14,15

14 Notwithstanding ye have well done, that ye did communicate with my affliction.

15 Now ye Philippians know also, that in the beginning of the gospel, when I departed from Macedonia, no church communicated with me as concerning GIVING AND RECEIVING, but ye only.

You need to underline in your Bible the phrase "giving and receiving." Notice it's giving *and* receiving. With God, there can never be giving without receiving. And there can never be receiving without giving.

PHILIPPIANS 4:16,17

16 For even in Thessalonica ye sent once and again unto my necessity.

17 Not because I desire a gift: but I desire fruit that may abound to your account.

Did you know that you can open accounts with God and make deposits? Those who make deposits into these accounts also have the right to make withdrawals.

Many people have accounts where they hide away money for emergencies. Hidden money, money which you are hiding for hard times, is a confession for hard times. You are confessing for hard times when you hide money for hard times! Pay attention and you will not have any financial difficulties. The Lord wants you to be willing to give it all. So tell God, "If You want it, let me know."

As we already saw, when your money touches the hands of God, it becomes supernatural—meaning it starts multiplying. The moment that it touches God's hands, there has to be a harvest, but the supernatural process begins when you first sow into the Kingdom. Your money touches the supernatural—in other words, five dollars is no longer five dollars. Five hundred is no longer five hundred—it could be anything. But it can never come back to you the same way it left. If it could, God wouldn't be God.

A Vision for Giving Into Good Soil

Where there is no vision, you have nowhere to sow. In other words, you can't just give to the lady down the street or into Wal Mart's hands and expect a multiplied harvest. If you're not sowing where God wants you to sow, that money will not be multiplied back to you supernaturally. You see, you sow with your spirit. When you put your money in God's hands, instantly, that money turns into supernatural money. There is not an amount you're dealing with anymore, and there are no limits.

PHILIPPIANS 4:18,19

18 But I have all, and abound: I am full, having received of Epaphroditus the things which were sent from you, an odour of a sweet smell, a sacrifice acceptable, wellpleasing to God.

19 But my God shall supply all your need according to his riches in glory by Christ Jesus.

When you open up an account with God—when you sow into His purposes—God becomes responsible for meeting your needs.

Fishes and Fragments

Looking back at the account of the multiplying of the loaves and fish in John chapter 6, notice that the purpose of the miracle of multiplying the fish and the bread was to meet the needs of the people. When the purpose was completed, Jesus said to the disciples, "...*Gather up the fragments that remain, that nothing be lost*" (John 6:12). I read that verse of Scripture, and the Lord said to me, "The house you live in and the car you drive are the 'fragments.'" So people who are arguing and complaining about those who are walking in covenant wealth, all they're arguing about is fragments!

God's purpose has already been fulfilled when you see fragments in a person's life—a lifestyle that has been changed. When a person is walking in covenant wealth, the money and material wealth he or she possesses is all just fragments. Those fragments came along after the purpose was fulfilled. When God uses someone to fulfill His purpose financially, the fragments belong to the one God uses. As I said before, who do you think took home those 12 baskets full of leftover bread and fish?

When people argue about someone's fragments, they are lacking understanding concerning the purpose. They don't know what happened to cause those fragments to show up in that person's life. They don't understand that when a purpose is fulfilled, God's blessings start flowing toward the individual He used.

Notice also from the account in John chapter 6 that the Lord did not serve the people himself. He gave thanks to God for that bread and fish, and as it started multiplying, He placed it in the disciples' hands. In the same way, God uses *our* hands to transfer His wealth into the earth realm. We who would be commanders of covenant wealth must realize that it's not about us, but about Him. We are simply vessels that He uses to fulfill His purposes. And from seedtime to the time of the miracle-multiplication harvest, God gets all the glory when the purpose is served and the fragments start showing up!

[1]For an in-depth study of this subject, see Dr. Thompson's book *You're Not Broke—You Have a Seed!*

Having the Right Mindset
for Miracle Money

There are three thoughts that must prevail in the life of one who walks in covenant wealth. *First,* he or she must believe in wealth as a part of the covenant and of the blessing of Abraham. You must believe it's all right to be blessed and to have nice things once you've fulfilled God's purposes with finances and have submitted to Him with your money.

The *second* mindset you must have to walk in covenant wealth is that you must align yourself with God and His Word concerning money. Whatever He says to do with your money is what you'll do. Wherever He tells you to sow money is where you'll sow it. However He tells you to think about money is how you'll think about it.

Third, you must be prepared in your heart and mind for persecutors and prosecutors who are ignorant of the truth and who will come against you. When you begin to walk in covenant wealth and your lifestyle begins to change, some people (and I'm talking about church people—

Christians who are bound by religious tradition) will talk against you. They'll say, for example, "Who does she think she is?" You can just say, "I *know* who I am. I am a child of the King." (If those people were smart, they would try to be rubbing elbows with you instead of talking about you.)

When you start walking in covenant wealth, you will become a sign and a wonder in your neighborhood, wherever you live. But you have to think correctly about wealth in order to walk in it. You cannot mix religious ideas with the revelation of wealth. If you do, you will contaminate the anointing that will bring wealth to pass in your life.

What does the Lord think about money? Let's look at Jesus' thoughts about money when He walked on the earth?

MARK 12:41

41 And Jesus sat over against the treasury, and beheld how the people cast money into the treasury: and many that were rich cast in much.

This seems strange for Jesus to sit in "church" and have His mind on the treasury. Today, people might say it is unscriptural or unbiblical—downright un-Christian!

Why would Jesus watch the treasury? He wasn't watching the choir; He was watching the treasury. He is the King of kings and Lord of lords, and He was watching the treasury. Why? We need to wake up to the fact that the treasury means something to God.

To function and operate in the earth realm, the loudest voice in the natural is money.

Let's look at that verse again in its context.

MARK 12:41-44

41 And Jesus sat over against the treasury, and beheld how the people cast money into the treasury: and many that were rich cast in much.

42 And there came a certain poor widow, and she threw in two mites, which make a farthing.

43 And he called unto him his disciples, and saith unto them, Verily I say unto you, That this poor widow hath cast more in, than all they which have cast into the treasury:

44 For all they did cast in of their abundance; but she of her want did cast in all that she had, even all her living.

One thing we can learn from this widow's giving is that if you really want to be used financially, the tithe in itself is not going to get it. Your freewill offering is not going to get it, and your sacrificial offering is not enough. If you really want to walk in the God-kind of wealth, you are going to have to come to the point of saying, "I own nothing and God owns everything." Then, as we've seen, you'll have to be ready to give as He directs, without question.

Really, in order to have covenant money, you have to separate yourself from money. Jesus cannot just be Lord over your spirit, soul, and body; He has to be Lord over your finances too. You have to come to the point where there is no limit to what you would do if God told you to do it. You are not afraid. If you really trust God—and you *can* trust God—you won't have a set amount that you'll give for Him. You will give it all.

Ask yourself if you really trust God with your finances and with your financial well-being. Are you willing to do what this widow did? Are you willing to trust God like she did? Are you ready for God to have full control of your finances—of *all* of your finances? It doesn't matter what you have or don't have—would you give it all?

As we read this account of the widow's giving her all, we usually get to comparing the rich with the poor. But grasp the importance of this sermon from Heaven! The good life is prearranged, preordained by God. Those who want to break out from this world's system of wealth and really walk in the fullness of God's financial plan will have to die to money.

There can't be any resurrection without a death. You have to die to money and die to things before there can be a resurrection of your finances. Let me say it like this: What you don't die to will not resurrect. Jesus said, *"Verily, verily, I say unto you, Except a corn of wheat fall into the ground and die, it abideth alone: but if it die, it bringeth forth much fruit"* (John 12:24).

The woman gave all she had. The Lord will make a request of you someday, and He won't want to hear about all your religious ideas and excuses. Money talks to God; your money is how God really finds you out. Anybody can holler, "Hallelujah!" But can he "put his money where his mouth is"?

Walking in covenant wealth is more than just tithing or saying, "Money cometh." You have to be sold out. You have to get your minds off things—off the fragments. The fragments come along with the job. The job that God will use you for will be the vision He has planted within you. And when God finds out that you are sold out to Him, He will let you have money.

Do you think that widow woman went unblessed? Do you think God forgot about her? The Bible didn't write everything, but I believe something special happened in her life when she sowed everything she had in that offering. If you could beat God in your giving, God would no longer be God. And we know that will never happen. He is the "exceeding abundantly above all you could ask or think" God (see Ephesians 3:20)!

74

The 'Unlimited' Return

There are ministers I've heard about who teach that there is a hundredfold return. Now, they don't mean to do it, but they are contradicting Jesus! And I will take Jesus' word before I'll take the word of even an anointed man or woman of God. I'm going to go with the Lord.

Let me explain, because if you're going to align yourself with God and His Word, you need to have the truth clear in your heart and mind that God is an unlimited God. Mark chapter 10 does deal with the hundredfold return. But God is not a 30-fold, 60-fold, or 100-fold God. The 30-, 60-, and 100-fold measurements are for us to know where we are. But God is an unlimited God, and you will have to get His "limitlessness" straight in your mind. There is no level at which you can "break" God or cause Him to go broke. And there is no level at which God stops when it comes to blessing us. That level is up to us, not Him.

Men are fighting the Church so badly concerning the preaching of financial prosperity. Many preachers are fighting it because they don't understand it. If they would just stay in their lane, keep driving the car that God gave them, so to speak, and go where God wants them to go, things would be so much better. Those preachers should just drive their car and let somebody else—some other minister—put the packages in their car!

When you get out of your lane, you mess up. You don't have any Scripture to back you up in your arguing. You're just arguing to be arguing! You get over into an area of ignorance, and ignorance is not bliss—*and it's not blessed*!

Jesus Himself told His disciples in Mark 10 that if they did what He told them to do, they would receive a hundredfold—a return on their giving—*now*, in this life (v. 30). I'm so glad Jesus said it. Some theologians would have said, "You will receive a return *later*." But if the Lord said it, He will surely do it for you in the here and now— and more besides if you'll learn to think like He does about covenant wealth.

Manifestation Secrets

M any in the Body of Christ know about making confessions based on the Word, but they aren't seeing the results that the Word promises them. Eventually, a confession of faith in God's Word should turn into a manifestation. If we don't set ourselves to agree that confessions should lead to manifestations, we will remain defeated, stuck in our "confession mode" with very little coming to pass in our lives in the way of a breakthrough.

I want to share with you a verse that holds the key to any type of manifestation you need in your life.

JOHN 14:21

21 He that hath my commandments, and keepeth them, he it is that loveth me: and he that loveth me shall be loved of my Father, and I will love him, AND I WILL MANIFEST MYSELF TO HIM.

In this verse, you are looking at the divine secret to receiving manifestations, because when the Lord said that He would manifest Himself, that means that any manifestation that is covered in the covenant becomes available to the believer who loves God and keeps His commandments. God will manifest His ways, His instructions, His leading, and His help—whatever you need in order to appropriate and enjoy for yourself the blessing of God.

Is it manifestation time in your life? You can receive manifestations, and the whole world will know about it. No satanic power will be able to stop it, and you won't be able to hide what God is doing in your life!

One of the keys to financial miracles—breakthroughs, increase, and abundance—is found in John 2:5: "Whatsoever He says to you, do it," referring to what Mary said to the disciples at the wedding at Cana, where Jesus turned the water into wine. When you begin to do this with what you have, your money problems will be all over.

I was in Kansas City, Missouri, years ago, ministering in the church of one of my sons in the faith. Bishop Jakes was also ministering, and while we were there, the Lord told me to buy him a pair of shoes. I didn't do it right then, but later on when I saw Bishop Jakes again, the Lord reminded me, so I approached him. Now I didn't know any better at the time, but I thought that $500 could get him a good pair of shoes. I said to him, "Bishop, will five hundred dollars buy you a nice pair of shoes?" He was very kind and courteous. He smiled and said, "Oh, yes." Then he bowed as he received the $500. About a week later, I received $10,500 unexpectedly. The Lord told me, "That's from your buying Bishop Jakes those shoes."

Things like that have happened to me more than once. You see, you don't pick the person; the Lord does. Remember, whatever *He* says to do, you do it.

Many people are looking to give to somebody who's broke. They don't believe in "upward sowing," where "the lesser blesses the greater"—where you're blessing some-body who has already been where you are, and his or her anointing can reverse your situation and pick you up.

So don't always look for somebody who is poor or down-and-out to give to. Listen to the Spirit of God, because God will use some people as soil for your sowing that will serve as your bouncing-off ground to walking in covenant wealth. For example, a woman you see might be out-dressing you, but if the Lord told you to give her $200, for example—even if her dress is better than your dress—give it to her quickly, because your wardrobe is about to change! God is setting you up for a breakthrough.

It all goes back to John 2:5, which says, ". . .*Whatsoever he saith unto you, do it*" You see, it didn't make sense to fill those water pots with water and then serve it to the guests as wine. And in the same way, God is not always going to deal with you in such a way that you can figure it out or in such a way that you're in control.

You can't be in control if you want to be a commander of covenant wealth. To be a commander, you have to submit first. You have to yield to Him. And once He finds out that you'll do it, He will let you have covenant money. But, as we saw, if you won't yield to Him now, in the little things, He knows what would happen if you were at the top of the lad-der in your finances. You wouldn't be in partnership with Him, and that is what God is looking for—partners!

You Are Not Alone in Your Situation or Circumstance

You can have faith to receive anything the Bible says you can have. We know that God is no respecter of persons (Acts 10:34). What He has ever done for anyone else, He will do for you too.

In the following verses, we can read here that Jesus was interested in Peter's paying taxes, and He made supernatural provision for him to be able to do it. What's more important is how Jesus identified with Peter in the paying of the taxes.

MATTHEW 17:24-27

24 And when they were come to Capernaum, they that received tribute money came to Peter, and said, Doth not your master pay tribute?

25 He saith, Yes. And when he was come into the house, Jesus prevented him, saying, What thinkest thou, Simon? of whom do the kings of the earth take custom or tribute? of their own children, or of strangers?

26 Peter saith unto him, Of strangers. Jesus saith unto him, Then are the children free.

27 Notwithstanding, lest we should offend them, go thou to the sea, and cast an hook, and take up the fish that first cometh up; and when thou hast opened his mouth, thou shalt find a piece of money: that take, and give unto them for me and thee.

What a miracle! The money Peter needed was in a fish's mouth! This is a classic example of the supernatural in manifestation. Your supernatural manifestation doesn't have to be in the mouth of a fish, but things of this nature will begin to happen on your behalf when God begins to set you up. Somebody will do something for you, and he won't know why he's doing it. But the anointing is calling for it, and he just happens to be the person God uses to do it.

I read verse 27 and thought the miracle was that the fish had money it its mouth. But the Lord said to me, "Read that verse again." *"Notwithstanding, lest we should offend them, go thou to the sea, and cast an hook, and take up the fish that first cometh up; and when thou hast opened his mouth, thou shalt find a piece of money: that take, and give unto them FOR ME AND THEE."*

Then I saw that the miracle is "for me and thee." I saw that when I am in debt, in a manner of speaking, *God* is in debt, and God wants me out of debt just as much as I want to get out, because I'm wearing His Name. Jesus said to Peter, "This miracle is not just for you, but for Me. Take this money and pay for you and Me."

You are not in your condition by yourself. The Lord is in it with you, and He is ready to eradicate from your life any symptom of lack. A miracle can happen in your life tomorrow or the next day—at any moment—as you learn to cooperate with the Spirit of God and keep the commandments, or the Word, of God.

More Principles of Manifestations

We looked at John 14:21, which says, *"He that hath my commandments, and keepeth them, he it is that loveth me: and he that loveth me shall be loved of my Father, and I will love him, and will manifest myself to him."* Now let's look at the two verses that follow.

JOHN 14:22,23

22 Judas saith unto him, not Iscariot, Lord, how is it that thou wilt manifest thyself unto us, and not unto the world?

23 Jesus answered and said unto him, If a man love me, he will keep my words: and my Father will love him, and we will come unto him, and make our abode with him.

First of all, the world cannot keep God's commandments. Matthew 13:11 tells us, *"…it is given unto you to know the mysteries of the kingdom of heaven, but to them it is not given."* The world is not given to know the mysteries, but we are. (I'll talk more about these mysteries in the next chapter.) Judas was really asking the question, "How am I going to know something the world doesn't know?" What he didn't realize was, he was *supposed* to know things the world couldn't know, because it had been given to him to know the mysteries.

There are three things from the Word you should know about manifestations that will encourage you in your faith.

1. Jesus never manifested Himself empty-handed. So if you keep His commandments and show your love toward Him, He and the Father will come and manifest themselves to you.

That means all of the benefits of the covenant come along with that manifestation!

2. Jesus will never show up and say, "I can't do that for you," if you have faith for it.

3. If you know the mysteries, you can have the manifestations.

Where can the mysteries be found? In the pages of the Word. And how do the manifestations come? By your obedience to the Word—by your keeping the commandments of God. When you practice obedience to God's Word in everything, you'll be ready when He speaks to you and tells you to do something. You'll be a speedy doer of John 2:5 so that whatever He says, you will indeed do it!

CHAPTER NINE

Miracle Insight and Mystery Understanding

It is very important to understand that in everything that God releases in the earth realm, He releases it in a mystery. And wealth for the Body of Christ is a mystery that you cannot tap into by religion. You cannot tap into it by tradition. The only way you can tap into the God-kind of wealth is by revelation.

We know the Scriptures. We can quote them. But there are certain mysteries about abundance that the Body of Christ has not walked in as yet. We are just easing into it a little bit now. But there is a group who are grasping these mysteries that God will use to finance the end-time harvest.

Supernatural debt-cancellation, supernatural increase, and living a supernatural life are mysteries. Many who have talked about them have never lived them. But the lifestyle of Abraham, Isaac, Jacob, Job, David, and Solomon is still available to the people of God. We can read in the Bible about the wealth that came upon the people who obeyed God. For example, the Bible says that Job was the greatest man in the East (Job 1:3).

In Chapter One, we talked about the importance of knowing God's will concerning wealth before you can lay hold of wealth and walk in it. We looked at several verses in the Old Testament and New Testament that reveal God's will about money. First Corinthians 2:9 is another verse that will help us understand that wealth is the will of God for us today.

1 CORINTHIANS 2:9

. . .Eye hath not seen, nor ear heard, neither have entered into the heart of man, the things which God hath prepared for them that love him.

Do you love God? If you do, you are a candidate for the wealth of God. Religion, theology, and the doctrines and traditions of men have tried to talk us out of it. Even the world says that since we're Christians, we shouldn't be concerned about where we live, what we drive, and all of that. And they try to cut off money from the Gospel. But God has given us the ability to understand the mysteries of covenant wealth, and we have to work those mysteries with the insight that God has given us.

It Is Given To You to Know the Mysteries of Covenant Wealth

In Matthew 13, after Jesus explained the Parable of the Sower, the disciples asked Him why He spoke to the crowds in parables.

MATTHEW 13:11

11 He answered and said unto them, Because it is given unto you to know the mysteries of the kingdom of heaven, but to them it is not given.

Something has been given to us as believers that non-believers do not have. Since that is so, our lives should be different than their lives. Here we see Jesus telling the disciples that it has been given unto them to know the mysteries of the Kingdom of Heaven—but that to others, it was not given. God wants us to know the mysteries of wealth, because He wants to reveal to us how to operate beyond natural standards.

The understanding of covenant wealth mysteries is available to the child of God. You don't have to depend on your job. You don't have to depend on your academic ability. There is a stronger dependency you can have—on your anointed ability. You can switch from academic living to anointed living in the world of financial freedom.

The Bible says it is given to you to know the mysteries. How does this work? Supernaturally.

MATTHEW 13:12

12 For whosoever hath, to him shall be given, and he shall have more abundance: but whosoever hath not, from him shall be taken away even that he hath.

Once we understand the mystery of wealth, Jesus said, "It shall be given to us in more abundance," because now we know how to tap into the supply that God wants us to handle for Him. It will happen to us when we have wisdom and revelation, and we work it from a spiritual perspective *without leaving our mind out*! In other words, we have to *think*! The Bible says we have the mind of Christ (1 Cor. 2:16), and let me tell you, Christ never thought about shortages. So we have to renew our minds and our thinking on the matter of wealth, because we have been religiously brainwashed concerning what God thinks about it.

We have to understand these mysteries and stop letting other voices stop us from walking in our covenant. We have to stop acting so super-spiritual, saying, "I'm not concerned about money."

You're a liar if you say that! You need some money if you're going to live life in this world! And it doesn't matter how well you can pray. When it comes to building a two-and-half-million-dollar project for the ministry, for example, prayer alone will not build it!

So I am going to take you into the world of unraveling the mysteries of your wealth. Your last name, your academic ability, and the color of your skin have nothing to do with what I'm going to show you. It is open to every believer who wants to walk in it.

Miracle Insight

What is miracle insight? It is insight about miracles—about how God and the Holy Spirit work to bring them about in your life. Miracle insight will produce miracle money, or money that you didn't work for. It could be a land deal you didn't ask for, for example. It is something the Lord just does for you. It is the grace, mercy, goodness, kindness, and power of God working on your behalf that no one can stop.

First, we need to know that mysteries have to be revealed to us by the Holy Spirit. So if we want mysteries revealed to us, we're going to have to make ourselves available to God. Then we will see what others don't see, because it has been given unto us to "...*know the mysteries of the kingdom of heaven*" (Matt. 13:11).

Jesus meant it when He said, "I have come that you might have life and might have it more abundantly" (John 10:10). It is given to you to know what Ephesians 3:20 means: "He is able to do exceeding abundantly above all that we ask or think" It is given to you to know what Jesus meant when He said, "Give and it shall be given unto you" (Luke 6:38).

It is given to us to know these revelations and mysteries. They are "coded" so that a natural man can't catch them but only those of us in the Word, because the entrance of His Word gives light (Ps. 119:130)—it gives light so that mysteries are no longer mysteries to us.

Divine Moments—
When Secrets Are Revealed

It is revealed to us in the Scriptures that there are certain things that are secret, But those things which God reveals to us are no longer a secret! These secrets revealed occur at "divine moments" when His Spirit pulls back the curtains while you're reading or meditating on a scripture, and you start seeing more than you've seen before.

"Divine moments" are times when God pulls back the curtains, so to speak, and gives you a peek into the reality of what you're believing Him for. And oftentimes, you'll see how it will come to pass. God asks, "Do you see it?" Then He shuts it back up. That moment was just for you.

Also, when you are praying in tongues, God can expose your spirit to divine truths that you could get no other way—not even by just reading the Bible. (Certainly, you have to constantly read and meditate on God's Word, the Bible. In fact, the Holy Spirit will never speak anything to you that doesn't line up with the Bible.)

ISAIAH 45:3

3 And I will give thee the treasures of darkness, and hidden riches of secret places, that thou mayest know that I, the Lord, which call thee by thy name, am the God of Israel.

Treasures and hidden riches have been hiding from you, but they will not be able to hide any longer because the anointing upon your life will shine the light upon the dark places so that you can see the mysteries of wealth and become enabled to walk in your rights and privileges as a covenant child of God.

DEUTERONOMY 29:29

29 The secret things belong unto the Lord our God: but those things which are revealed belong unto us and to our children for ever, that we may do all the words of this law.

Those things that are revealed belong to us and to our children forever. That means that once God reveals something to us, He won't take it back. You can walk therein, and no man, no foe, no principality, and no power can stop you from walking in it. When revelation on how to get out of debt comes, Satan's heyday that he has been having in your life will be over. A secret has been revealed to you by the anointing, and debt is over and done with; it's gone, and it is just a matter of time before that fact will manifest and be apparent in your life.

PSALM 25:14

14 The secret of the Lord is with them that fear him; and he will shew them his covenant.

The secret of the Lord is with them who fear him, and He will show them His covenant. Do you know what it means if God begins to show you His covenant, His secrets? He gives us revelation knowledge of these things so that we can walk in them.(In the next chapter, we'll look in-depth at the role of the prophet in revealing these divine secrets.)

I have come to the point where I am a commander of wealth and money obeys me. Silver and gold obey me. But to get to this place, I had to learn to make myself available to God so He could give me revelation of the mysteries of the Scripture concerning wealth. I had to seek Him and believe Him for divine moments in which I could gain insight into the mysteries of money that had been hidden from me before.

After you experience one of these divine moments, your condition may stay the same, but your status automatically changes! In a divine moment, you will see something out of the ordinary. And it will become real in your spirit.

We're going to read about Joshua's visitation from the Lord, and I want you to think about finances when you're reading these scriptures.

JOSHUA 6:1,2

1 Now Jericho was straitly shut up because of the children of Israel: none went out, and none came in.

2 And the Lord said unto Joshua, See, I have given into thine hand Jericho, and the king thereof, and the mighty men of valour.

After this divine moment with God, Jericho's walls didn't mean a thing to Joshua anymore, although they were still standing. The Lord told Joshua "See, I have given into your hand Jericho and the king thereof and the mighty men of valor." That meant that, really, it was all over at that moment!

Your finances may be "straitly shut up" as was the city of Jericho. But in a divine moment with God, He will show you that He has already dealt with every wall. And when you see and act like you know it, then just as Jericho's walls fell, everything that has hindered you financially is going to fall too!

Your finances may have been shut up for 10, 15, or 20 years, but you need to shout! Faith shouts while the walls are still up! See yourself as financially free while that wall is still standing. Shout because the things that you're believing God for are coming to pass in your life!

May you have a divine moment in which you see yourself financially free and all of your needs met. You can't dream any bigger than God can deliver!

Mysteries That Can Bring You Out of Misery

The mystery of covenant wealth, in essence, is very simple. The secret is in obeying God. It is in being faithful over a few things so that He can make you ruler over many (Matt. 25:21). God wants us to understand this and *all* the mysteries that will bring us out of our misery. There is a lot of misery in the Body of Christ. We've got a shout. We've got a praise. We know how to worship Him. We know how to intercede. But there is a lot of misery, because most Christians don't know how to get their breakthrough.

We have a right to know the mysteries. We have a right to be blessed. We have a right to be the head and not the tail. We have a right to live in a beautiful home. This kind of thinking bothers Satan. He doesn't want us to know the mysteries, because we have a grave responsibility with money to preach the Gospel.

But when the mysteries of money get cleared up in your thinking, living a good life and supporting the Kingdom of God on a high level will be your reality. When you realize how much God wants you to have and you start thinking in terms of "overflow," "abundance," and "more than enough" instead of "lack," "not enough," or even "barely enough," covenant wealth will no longer be a mystery in your life. Your mind will become illuminated to the mysteries of wealth. You will have an empowered mindset and mentality that will not allow you to think about your former condition, because you'll *know that you know* that you don't belong in that condition anymore! And every stronghold in your life that the enemy has tried to hold up against you will come down through your understanding of the mysteries.

Covenant Wealth and the Prophet's Ministry

The enemy has always tried to put enmity between the pulpit and the pew, between the minister and church members, so that people wouldn't recognize the gift that God is trying to give them.

God uses human agents. You have to understand that. You can pray all you want—God still uses human agents to get messages across to you. God has not changed His mind. He set it up that way in the Bible (Eph. 4:11-13), and that is still the way He does it. If the respect and the honor are not there, when the word comes forth, you won't be able to receive it because you are shut up or closed off in your spirit through a lack of respect for the pulpit.

This lack of esteem is the very thing that causes us to lag behind concerning covenant wealth. When God puts a word from Heaven into a minister's mouth, that word has the power to elevate you—to snatch you off welfare, off living on credit, off sickness and disease, and off bondage of any kind.

A minister of the Gospel can be anointed to call forth increase in your life in the Name of Jesus. As a representative of the Most High God, he or she can call you out of debt, lack, sickness, and disease. But you have to have a certain respect for the anointing and for God's ministers, or you will not benefit from it.

The Place of the Prophet in Commanding Wealth

In the Bible, everybody we see who was set free financially had a prophet speak into his or her life or had a prophetic word from God. Look at the widow of one of the sons of the prophets, for example, who was in so much debt, her debtors were going to come and take her children (see Seconds Kings 4:1-7). Who spoke into her life and caused her situation to be turned around completely? A prophet.

When another widow, in Zarephath, was gathering those sticks to cook her last meal and die because there was a famine in the land, who spoke to her and caused everything to change (see First Kings 17:8-16)? A prophet.

And when Jehoshaphat had five armies coming against him, and he didn't know what to do, who spoke into his life? A prophet. And how did that fight end? The Bible says they had so much spoils, it took three days to gather it—because God sent a prophet to tell them, "The battle is not yours, but Mine" (2 Chron. 20:15).

It is important that we esteem the ministry of the prophet. I want to show you a few things in this chapter and the next about the covenant blessings that can come into your life through a prophet being sent on a special mission to you by God. When you fear the Lord, He will show you His covenant through the ministry of a prophet.

There are various anointings in the Body of Christ for particular aspects of the covenant. We must tap into these anointings to receive full results. On every subject covered by the covenant, God has called particular men and women and has anointed them in that area. These men and women bear an anointing, and if you tap into that particular anointing, that part of the covenant will manifest itself in your life.

A Messenger or Just a Message?

It is very crucial that you understand that a *message about finances* and a *messenger of finances* are two different things. All ministers teach messages about finances because that is part of our job. But there are those whom God has chosen as messengers of His covenant of finances, and the anointing is different. For instance, there are messages about healing, but Benny Hinn is a messenger of healing. He is just one whom God has specially anointed to minister healing. God anointed him for that message and, therefore, he gets plenty of results—more so than the man or woman who isn't called particularly to minister healing.

You may have heard many messages and read many scriptures on finances, but when a messenger of finances comes on the scene, it totally changes the atmosphere of the meeting. At any moment, anything can happen in the realm of the Spirit, *supernaturally*, on your behalf.

The Prophet Completes the Mystery

In the last chapter, we looked at miracle insight and mystery understanding as keys to walking in covenant wealth. I said that everything God releases in the earth realm, He releases it in a mystery. And wealth for the Body of Christ is a mystery that we can tap into by revelation—by our understanding of the mystery.

You will not find your completion of the mystery by yourself. You need a prophet of God to open it up for you in a divine way. There are some things the Holy Spirit will not tell you without a prophet. So, certainly, you can receive certain revelation and understanding through your study of the Word—and you *should* study the Word of God—but the completion of the mysteries will come through a man or woman of God. You will never just study your way out.

God will not permit you to bypass the one He has sent. God's system is set up for apostles, prophets, evangelists, pastors, and teachers to equip believers (Eph. 4:11-13). That is why the devil has been a teaser and a tantalizer in this area. And he has been largely successful in separating the pulpit and the pew, as I talked about at the beginning of this chapter.

AMOS 3:7

7 Surely the Lord God will do nothing, but he revealeth his secret unto his servants the prophets.

You see, there are certain secrets that God reveals to His prophets. And the full mystery of the covenant can't be revealed to you unless you permit God to reveal it to you through His prophets. When a prophet speaks to you and you are receptive, you will hear words that will give you insight that you never had before and that complete the revelation knowledge you've already received from God.

Understanding the mysteries of the covenant releases covenant abundance in your life. Along with your study, a prophet's speaking to you can cause the mysteries to become revelation, and then the rain of abundance—of having more than enough—comes. But you will never fully know the mystery without the prophet.

Pastors must teach this to their congregations. The congregation's word of completion is in the prophet's mouth. When a prophet opens his mouth, it is time to listen intently and to esteem the word from God that he or she brings forth. One word from God can make your troubles history.

It has been given to us to know the mysteries of the Kingdom of Heaven (Matt. 13:11), as we saw in the last chapter. We can receive for ourselves revelation of the mysteries from God. But the revelation that we receive combined with the word from the mouth of the prophet will put us in a different category where receiving from God is concerned.

In order to be a commander of covenant wealth, the mystery has to be revealed to you by the Holy Spirit. Then the next step to take is to receive the completion of the mystery through a prophetic word—through the mouth of a prophet. If you make yourself available to him and to hearing God's voice through him, you will begin to see things others don't see and to walk in things others don't walk in. And the rain of abundance will flood your life quickly and release you to become a commander of covenant wealth.

How to Receive

a Prophetic Breakthrough

There are five things you will have to do if you're going to receive your breakthrough and be released to walk in covenant wealth. *Number one*, you will have to receive proper prophetic instruction and obey it, as we will study in-depth in this chapter.

Number two, you will have to be a seeker of the Kingdom of God and its affairs and agendas. We covered this truth previously in this book. In order to walk in covenant wealth, you have to know the purpose for wealth, and you have to be sold out to God's will—to Kingdom purposes.

Number three, you will have to understand the power of stewardship. You see, where you are now will set you up for the next level. In other words, as we've seen, you can't wait to get wealth before you decide to sow seed. You have to sow now—right where you are now financially—if you're going to be a steward of money for God and become a commander of covenant wealth.

The *number four* thing you'll need to do to receive a prophetic breakthrough is to consistently proclaim wealth as part as God's divine plan for you. All the money in the world moves when you say, "Money cometh!" from a heart of faith. When you say those words, you enter into the realm of the supernatural, and it has worldwide effects. There could be money coming to you in the United States from Germany, for example, when the Holy Spirit and the angels of God hear you speak forth that supernatural call.

Don't ever stop saying, "Money cometh to me *now*!" When you say those words, a supernatural, prophetic anointing for wealth comes upon you. "Money cometh" is not a slogan or cliché. It is not a fad or trend. It's a prophetic command that, coming out of your heart and mouth, will effect a change in your life and circumstances.[1]

"Well, how long do I say it?" you might ask. Say it until supernatural finances start rolling into your house and overflow in your life.

I am a living example of what those words will do for you. I was a farm boy growing up. I went to high school, but I didn't go to college. However, not one of my class-mates can out-live me financially. And every one of my relatives who are professional people must understand that degrees cannot deal with the divine. Some of my rela-tives get irritated at times. But they have only to ask me, and I will tell them how I'm doing it. I'll say, "God is doing it for me, because I am in covenant with Him."

Number five, to receive a prophetic breakthrough, you will have to take full hold of the abundant lifestyle Jesus desires and has made possible for your life. In other words, as we saw in Chapter One, you need to be fully persuaded from the Word that wealth is the will of God for you!

Receiving and Obeying Prophetic Instruction

In the last chapter, I used the example of King Jehoshaphat as someone who sought instruction from God which came to Jehoshaphat through the mouth of God's prophet.

In Second Chronicles 20, we can read that five kings were assembled against Jehoshaphat. He had prayed and fasted and had reached the point where he said to the Lord, "I don't know what to do. But I have my eyes on you" (v. 12). When Jehoshaphat was in that situation, God moved on a prophet and gave the prophet divine instructions for Jehoshaphat. And we know that Jehoshaphat received and obeyed the prophetic instruction, and he received a prophetic breakthrough as a result.

2 CHRONICLES 20:20

20 And they rose early in the morning, and went forth into the wilderness of Tekoa: and as they went forth, Jehoshaphat stood and said, Hear me, O Judah, and ye inhabitants of Jerusalem; Believe in the Lord your God, SO SHALL YE BE ESTABLISHED; believe his prophets, SO SHALL YE PROSPER.

Following prophetic instruction is very important to walking in covenant wealth. God said that if you believed His prophets, you would prosper. Matthew 10:41 is a scripture that is often misunderstood by many, but after we study it and believe it, we can move on to our territory and possess that which is ours.

Pay attention to what this verse is saying.

MATTHEW 10:41

41 He that receiveth a prophet in the name of a prophet shall receive a prophet's reward; and he that receiveth a righteous man in the name of a righteous man shall receive a right-eous man's reward.

Five armies came against Jehoshaphat and the children of Israel, but they believed the prophet, and they received a prophet's reward.

2 CHRONICLES 20:25

25 And when Jehoshaphat and his people came to take away the spoil of them, they found among them in abundance both riches with the dead bodies, and precious jewels, which they stripped off for themselves, more than they could carry away: and they were three days in gathering of the spoil, it was so much.

Operating by prophetic instructions can cause you to advance quickly in the realm of the Spirit. That is exactly what happened here. One day it looked bad, and the next day all of their enemies were down. One day they were broke, and the next day they were gathering more wealth than they could carry away! So you can see how important it is to receive and act on prophetic instruction.

Second Chronicles 20:20 says, "...*Believe in the Lord your God, SO SHALL YE BE ESTABLISHED; believe his prophets, SO SHALL YE PROSPER.*" The problem is, we've been believing God, and God has brought us to *establishment.* But God's way is to take us on to *prosperity,* and He does that through men and women He has anointed. If you ignore those men and women, all you can be is established. You will be established in the truth, all right, but you won't prosper in the truth in the way that God intends. You won't receive His highest and best.

Second Chronicles 20:20 says that if you believe God's prophets, you shall prosper. It doesn't say you *might* prosper;

it says you *shall* prosper! Nobody can stop it. When you have found a strong man or woman of God, you have found a jewel. Don't take his or her words lightly. Once you receive a prophetic revelation, it can't be taken from you if you will not let it go. There is no foe, no power, that can stand against you, because God sent the message.

God is ready to manifest Himself in your life with your promised covenant wealth. You are an heir of God, a joint-heir with Christ (Gal. 4:7), and you have a right to be debt-free. God is the same God that blessed Abraham, Isaac, and Jacob through the covenant.

God is not a man that He can lie. If He says it, He will make it good (Num. 23:19). When God sends His Word to you, it will prosper in that for which He sent it (Isa. 55:11). That Word will bring a fire into you than will lead you out of every kind of trouble and bondage.

A Prophetic Word Can Release You From Financial Captivity

God wants to break you out of financial captivity—out of bondage to debt and lack. Lack is one of the most damnable things on the face of the earth to hinder a person from doing what the Lord told him or her to do. The devil tries to lock us up so deep in debt that we can hardly pray sometimes. I've been there, done that—I know what I'm talking about. But I know the way out, too, and I am declaring that way to you!

JEREMIAH 33:6,7

6 Behold, I will bring it health and cure, and I will cure them, and will reveal unto them the abundance of peace and truth.

7 And I will cause the captivity of Judah and the captivity of Israel to return, and will build them, as at the first.

Financial captivity is a very strong bondage in the Church. We have a tendency in the Church to have a *false prosperity*, which is having things with no money—or having things on credit—and putting on a prosperous front, acting like we have wealth when we don't.

JEREMIAH 33:8,9

8 And I will cleanse them from all their iniquity, whereby they have sinned against me; and I will pardon all their iniquities, whereby they have sinned, and whereby they have transgressed against me.

9 And it shall be to me a name of joy, a praise and an honour before all the nations of the earth, which shall hear all the good that I do unto them: and they shall fear and tremble for all the goodness and for all the prosperity that I procure unto it.

These are powerful scriptures. When God begins to manifest His covenant in your life, it will cause your neighbors to tremble.

We are supposed to rise up and proclaim with our lives the goodness of the Lord. We are supposed to be an example. Our God is our Example; therefore, we have to position ourselves so that He can do on our behalf what He said in His Word He would do. I'm not just talking about what the Bible says; I'm talking about getting what the Bible says actually manifested in our lives!

Let's look briefly at the Israelites' deliverance from the bondage of Egypt. The Israelites were slaves in Egypt. They were shut up tight in their finances, and they needed a breakthrough.

HOSEA 12:13

13 And by a prophet the Lord brought Israel out of Egypt, and by a prophet was he preserved.

God brought them out by a prophet. But let's look at the condition they were in when He brought them out of their captivity.

PSALM 105:37-41

37 He brought them forth also with silver and gold: and there was not one feeble person among their tribes.

38 Egypt was glad when they departed: for the fear of them fell upon them.

39 He [the Lord] *spread a cloud for a covering; and fire to give light in the night.*

40 The people asked, and he brought quails, and satisfied them with the bread of heaven.

41 He opened the rock, and the waters gushed out; they ran in the dry places like a river.

God brought them out rich and strong! As I mentioned previously, in Deuteronomy 8, God was talking to people whom He had made rich—they would probably be considered multimillionaires by today's standards. God was reminding them, "You have this wealth because I gave you the power to get it. Now, *remember* that it was I who gave you that."

Well, how did they get their wealth? Well, for one, they borrowed from the wicked as they were being delivered from Egypt. Moses got a prophetic word and told them,

"Go over there and borrow from the Egyptians. They're going to let it go because God's favor is upon you." So they borrowed from the wicked and left with all of their stuff (Exod. 12:35,36)!

A Biblical Example of Supernatural Debt-Cancellation

Do you believe in supernatural debt-cancellation? God supernaturally cancelled the Israelites' debt. They borrowed supernaturally and left Egypt. And when they stood before the Red Sea with their enemy pursuing them to get them and their stuff back, the sea opened up and the children of Israel made their way out of debt, out of lack, out of having just enough! They went through that water on dry land and came out on the other side. When Pharaoh and his army went down into that water, the water came down over them—and the Israelites' debt was cancelled at that moment. I mean, whom were they going to pay!

God has always used His prophets to give instruction to His people to show them the way out of where they were and into where He wanted them to be. That's why you have to have proper prophetic instruction to receive a breakthrough. The prophetic anointing will bring you through something before you know it, because there's an unction there to push you forward. A word from God and proper prophetic instructions will propel you into the place that God has prepared for you.

When God anoints somebody for a certain area of ministry, when he or she is speaking into people's lives, a "mantle" is imparted; something is released over them. There comes the capability of invoking the Presence of God to completely satisfy whatever need you have in your life.

'Instruction From God That Set Me on the Path, Charted My Course, and Prepared Me for Destiny!'

Years ago, I had a good job working at a plant. But one day, the Lord said to me, "Tomorrow is your day. You're quitting."

At the time the Lord said that, my wife and I were flat broke! I was making good money, but we were deep in debt. We had bills to pay, but I knew I had heard from Heaven. I went into my boss's office the next day with a suit on and said, "I have to quit. I know I'm supposed to give notice, but I don't have time."

That was all I really knew. When my boss asked me, "What are you going to do?" at first, I didn't know what to say. But just then, right on the spot, the Lord gave me the words. I said, "I can no longer take orders from two headquarters. The Lord told me to take all my orders from Him, and He would take care of me."

Now I know my boss felt sorry for me—a little black boy quitting his good job, with a wife and children at home to take care of. He thought I had gone crazy! But in time, the Lord fixed it so that he moved down the street from me. You could put his house—and it is a nice house—inside my house six times and still have room to walk around. And often, when he is driving to work, I'm sitting out on my porch rocking. I wave to him as he drives by. And it's all because a Man called Jesus came on my job and said, "Tomorrow is your day."

You may think those were natural events, but they were supernatural. The word of the Lord produced something powerful in my life because I obeyed it, and the word of the Lord to you will produce for you too!

I will tell you how powerful a prophetic word from God can be when you obey it from a heart of faith. When you're anointed to prosper and you're walking in covenant wealth, people who don't even like you will give to you! A man once brought a bag of money to my house who I *know* didn't like me. But he said, "The Lord told me to bring this to you. I took it, and as he was leaving, he turned around and said, "There's more where that came from."

In my ministry today, I have prophetic instructions from God concerning financial wealth and prosperity that He wants brought to the Body of Christ. God told me that wrong doctrines, beliefs, and traditions have to be pulled down in people's lives before they will receive from Him like He wants them to receive.

In Mark 7:13, Jesus said that the traditions of men made the Word of God of none effect. What are traditions of men? They are things that people hold on to, such as religious thinking and teaching that don't line up with the Bible, and it holds them back from getting their breakthrough.

The Law of Association and Environment— Influences That Can Affect Your Walking in the Covenant

I don't hang around people who think like that, and you shouldn't, either. The law of association demands that you watch whom you hang with, because whatever is on them will rub off on you—for good or for bad. For example, Abraham's anointing rubbed off on Lot. The Bible says that Abraham and Lot had so much that they couldn't stay in the same place. I wonder where Lot got his wealth? God didn't tell Lot leave anything; He told Abraham. And Abraham's blessing rubbed off on Lot.

I am a prophet of prosperity. I have declared prosperity to "rub off" on people, and I have seen it happen in amazing ways as they have cooperated with the principles and laws I share in this book. I see a restoration coming to the Body of Christ. I see the devil returning everything he has stolen from us. I see the devil with his hands up, returning your stuff, saying, "I don't want any trouble out of you.

Take your stuff back!" The devil had been holding you up, but now you are going to hold *him* up!

God wants me to declare to you that your financial battle is not yours; it is the Lord's. So stop trying to handle it yourself. Instead, yield to the Spirit of God and to the anointing. Just as Jeshoshaphat prayed in Second Chronicles 20:12, we can say with him, "*...our eyes are upon thee*"!

Divine Mercy on Your Money

As I said, I am a messenger of finances. And I declare that the Body of Christ is coming out of all forms of their financial Egypt—struggling, stress, poverty, and lack. Roadblocks to their financial wealth and well-being are being torn down. Strongholds in their thinking that have caused them to hold on to money where the Church is concerned are coming down! Money cometh to the Body of Christ! From this time forth, there is coming a divine mercy upon the finances of the Body of Christ.

What is divine mercy? For one, it is forgiveness where mistakes have been made financially. The devil has been holding some people back because they've missed it, and now they feel they deserve to struggle. They think they deserve to be in the situation they're in.

But God will forgive you for the mistakes you've made. He desires to bring healing and restoration to your finances so that they will no longer be shaken. They will no longer be influenced by the enemy but by the mercy, the grace, and the power of God. Not only will the Body of Christ leave their financial Egypt, they will take hold of the grace of God never to go back into bondage again! They will not accept or tolerate another financial situation like that another day in their life!

It sounds amazing, but you can get to the place in God where you will never have another financial problem in your life. As a child of the covenant, you can command wealth, and wealth will obey you. In the Name of Jesus, you can take authority over every harassing spirit that has been tormenting and bothering you in your finances. You can not only come out of "Egypt," you can come out preserved! Strong and rich, you can come of your Egypt and enter into your promised land!

Divine mercy is on your finances. You have been delivered and healed financially. Take hold of that in your spirit and receive it by faith. It doesn't matter how bad your finances are—you can get to the place where you'll never be broke another day in your life! So stop *thinking* broke. Stop saying what you don't have, and quit lying, saying you don't care about having nice stuff, because the nature of God in you should be comfortable, not *un*comfortable, with nice things.

The Body of Christ has been tithing and sowing, but now it is time for God to come through! Just one word from God can break the financial barriers and cause money to start coming your way. I decree that all of your tithes and every seed that you have sown will begin to manifest as never before in your life. I make a demand on the power of wealth on your behalf. In the Name of Jesus, I declare that your financial struggles are over! They're history!

I am making these decrees as a prophet of God with a message from God on financial wealth. Remember, Hosea 12:13 says that by a prophet, the Lord brought Israel out of Egypt, and by a prophet, Israel was preserved When the Lord brings you out, you are brought out to *stay* out! You are never going back again!

I hope that will be your lot today. Will you receive it? Will you do what it takes to receive your breakthrough and become a commander of covenant wealth?

In review, there are five steps to receiving your prophetic breakthrough:

1. You will have to receive proper prophetic instruction and obey it.

2. You will have to be a seeker of the Kingdom of God and its affairs and agendas.

3. You will have to understand the power of stewardship.

4. You will have to consistently proclaim wealth as part as God's divine plan for you.

5. You will have to fully take hold of the abundant lifestyle Jesus desires and has made possible for your life.

Allow the Spirit of God to set you up for a breakthrough as you put into practice these breakthrough laws and principles. You can receive prophetic instruction from the pages of this book that has the power to release you from every bondage concerning money and to set you, too, on a new course headed toward a new destiny.

[1]For an in-depth study of the revelation of "Money cometh," see Dr. Thompson's book *Money Cometh to the Body of Christ!*

Becoming a Wealth-Commanding Money Magnet for God!

I remember years ago when God first spoke to me and told me that He was making me a "money magnet." I'd never heard that term before, and I've been in the Body of Christ for more than 30 years. But the Lord revealed this to me. And it doesn't matter how becoming a money magnet sounds. I have confirmed that it came to me from God. And I'm not intimidated by what other people say. I am on a mission; I have a job to get done.

The Lord said to me, "I want you to start teaching on receiving power to become a money magnet." So I did, and I will include in this chapter a brief overview of this teaching.

First, as we saw in a previous chapter, you have to have Kingdom business on your mind to become a money magnet. When you're a money magnet for the Kingdom of God, you can be trusted with the "more-than-enough" kind of wealth—*covenant* wealth. Becoming a money magnet is simply qualifying to "wear" a financial anointing. Becoming a money magnet means you are walking in the commanding power of Jesus; you have His ability—His authority, anointing, and His favor—to command wealth.

When you have the favor of God on you for finances, it is a divine influence on your life. The favor of God places a divine influence on you that also grants special privileges to you. When you have the favor of God on you, you become an attraction.

I own a Rolls Royce, and some people haven't gotten over that fact yet! But if that bothers you, you couldn't have lived during the time Abraham was living. You would have died of a heart attack because of all the servants Abraham had behind him! And then during the time of Solomon, you wouldn't have ever gone to church. You would have fallen away, offended, because Solomon's crowd would have taken up the whole front row! You see, you can't have a problem with others' blessings and expect to be blessed yourself.

We have been respecting money, but as wealth-commanding money magnets for the Kingdom of God, *money* will begin to respect *us*! Money has lost respect for the Body of Christ. Money has forgotten who it belongs to. Silver and gold belong to us to get the job done that we've been assigned to do. The world system has to let our money go, because we have an assignment to complete—we have people to get saved, delivered, healed, and we have to feed the hungry, put clothes on the naked, and shelter people without homes.

Walking the Walk: Purity and Plenteousness

Let's look at some things we can specifically expect as we're walking in our covenant of wealth.

DEUTERONOMY 30:9

9 And the Lord thy God will make thee plenteous in every work of thine hand, in the fruit of thy body, and in the fruit of thy cattle, and in the fruit of thy land, for good: for the Lord will again rejoice over thee for good, as he rejoiced over thy fathers.

DEUTERONOMY 15:6

6 For the Lord thy God blesseth thee, as he promised thee: and thou shalt lend unto many nations, but thou shalt not borrow; and thou shalt reign over many nations, but they shall not reign over thee.

Deuteronomy 15:6 says, *"...thou shalt lend unto many nations, but thou shalt not borrow...."* You are bound by your anointing to be the lender. Remember I said that you have the ability to walk in this kind of wealth. But with this ability, there has to be purity. In other words, your motives have to right and you have to be right. You can't walk in sin and walk in the God-kind of wealth at the same time.

"Plenty" is our inheritance. But along with having plenty, there must be purity. You have to live a consecrated life. So let the Holy Ghost take your life over. Bring your body into subjection (1 Cor. 9:27), because holiness and prosperity go together. You can do it, but you have to be "dead" as Paul said in Galatians 2:20:*"I am crucified with Christ: nevertheless I live; yet not I, but Christ liveth in me: and the life which I now live in the flesh I live by the faith of the Son of God, who loved me, and gave himself for me."*

Do You Have a Problem With Plenty?

Some people don't have a problem with purity, but they do have a problem with plenty. But, really, if having plenty bothers them, that is a sure sign that their minds have not been renewed with the Word of God. They don't see wealth as God sees it. Therefore, they have some cleaning up of their minds to do!

PROVERBS 3:9,10

9 Honour the Lord with thy substance, and with the first-fruits of all thine increase:

10 So shall thy barns be filled with PLENTY, and thy presses shall burst out with new wine.

What does verse 10 say? "So shall thou wait for the first of the month so you can finally do a little something"? No, it says, *"So shall thy barns be filled with plenty..."*!

There are some who say, "You don't need all that money." But there are others of us who know that our God is bigger than the way we've been living. And I am tired of messing around! I'm ready for God to come through and show Himself strong on our behalf!

I have all kinds of "toys." Some people may have a problem with my having them, but those people weren't there when my wife and I gave a family a house paid in full. They weren't there when we sowed more money into the Kingdom than they make in a year—or even five years. And we've done it more than once. We sow often, and we sow bountifully, because we're commanders of covenant wealth.

Some people have a problem with plenty. But, really, there's not going to be any voting about it. It is already sealed by the blood of Jesus! So we're going to deal with it. Some people who are bound by religion will act like they believe in this message, but deep down, when they really get right down to it, they are fearful that it is not of God. Revelation knowledge is the only thing that will set them free.

Proverbs 10:22 says, *"The blessing of the Lord, it maketh rich, and he addeth no sorrow with it."* What will make you rich? The blessing of the Lord will make you rich. I have a question for you. Is there any power strong enough to stop the blessings of God in your life? Doubt and unbelief are the only two things that can stop the blessings of the Lord. The devil cannot stop your blessing; only you can stop it.

Pay careful attention to what Paul said in Ephesians 1, because revelation knowledge will cure any doubt and unbelief that's trying to hang around in your life.

EPHESIANS 1:15-23

15 Wherefore I also, after I heard of your faith in the Lord Jesus, and love unto all the saints,

16 Cease not to give thanks for you, making mention of you in my prayers;

17 That the God of our Lord Jesus Christ, the Father of glory, may give unto you the spirit of wisdom and revelation in the knowledge of him:

18 The eyes of your understanding being enlightened; that ye may know what is the hope of his calling, and what the riches of the glory of his inheritance in the saints,

19 And what is the exceeding greatness of his power to usward who believe, according to the working of his mighty power,

20 Which he wrought in Christ, when he raised him from the dead, and set him at his own right hand in the heavenly places,

21 Far above all principality, and power, and might, and dominion, and every name that is named, not only in this world, but also in that which is to come:

22 And hath put all things under his feet, and gave him to be the head over all things to the church,

23 Which is his body, the fulness of him that filleth all in all.

You can pray this prayer for yourself, and I encourage you to do so. If you still have any misgivings concerning money or if you're afraid of money, you need to get your eyes opened to the truth of God's Word.

Look at what Paul had to say in Ephesians chapter 2 concerning the fullness of redemption that Christ purchased for us.

EPHESIANS 2:4-7

4 But God, who is rich in mercy, for his great love wherewith he loved us,

5 Even when we were dead in sins, hath quickened us together with Christ, (by grace ye are saved;)

6 And hath raised us up together, and made us sit together in heavenly places in Christ Jesus:

7 That in the ages to come he might shew the exceeding riches of his grace in his kindness toward us through Christ Jesus.

If you're in the Body of Christ, you are legally and positionally far above debt, far above lack, far above poverty, far above any works of the devil. But you have to know it and act like it's true for it to produce something in your life.

I have no bills that come in my mailbox, no junk mail trying to lure me into buy something—only money comes in my mailbox! You have to see the environment of your mailbox changing! You have to see lack leaving you. You do it with the eye of faith and with your confession—with your believing and speaking.

You might be overwhelmed by your circumstances. But adverse circumstances don't bother me. I have a strong, strong anointing in the area of finances. I have no respect for poverty, lack, or for demons that may try to hold you back. I have no respect for your bills—it doesn't matter how much you owe. Those things don't move me. I can see debt-cancellation happening in your life. Now I'm not making light of what you may be going through. I understand the feelings of weakness that come with debt. But I also know that the covenant is stronger than anything! And I see you coming out of weakness and debt!

When you are wearing this type of covenant wealth anointing, money respects you, and you get to a point where you can't even *"think"* broke! That's where I am, and I want to see you get to that place too.

Let me explain what I mean by not even being able to think broke. I bought my wife a three-wheel motor bike. I paid about $20,000 for it, but I couldn't get her to ride it. I had been coaxing her for almost a year and a half to ride it, and, finally, one day, she got on it. We rode about 25 miles, and I was a happy man!

As I was riding behind her on my two-wheel motor bike, I thought to myself, *Why can't we have two three-wheelers, so I can ride a three-wheeler with her?* I have several bikes, but none was a three-wheeler. So I took the one that I was riding to a shop to have it converted to a three-wheeler.

I walked into the place and asked a man if he could convert it. The man said, "Yes, I could do it for ten thousand dollars." I said, "Get to putting the wheel on it." I didn't say, "I don't know if I want to do it," because I went there for the purpose of having the bike converted, and the price didn't make a difference in how soon I could get it done. That's the power of money. That's the power of covenant wealth.

Now, my brother or sister in the Lord, I believe that's where you're headed too! But you have to respect the covenant before the covenant will respect you. Those who don't permit God to come through because of the covenant are actually disrespecting the covenant.

Did you know that you're a misfit in the Kingdom of God if you let some denominational warrior or religious handicap hold you back from walking in the fullness of your covenant so that God can get His job done in the earth?

When you become a money magnet, your income is no longer the check from your job that you get on Friday or the first of the month. When you become a money magnet, money is unlimited; it comes from everywhere.

I have come to the point in my life and ministry that I can't even *think* about something too long before I have it. (I didn't say *confess* it; I can't even *mention* a thing too much, because if I mention it, it will pop up on the scene.) I have to be really careful about what I think about, because Ephesians 3:20 has manifested in my life so many times: *"Now unto him that is able to do exceeding abundantly above all that we ask or think, according to the power that worketh in us."*

When you get your spirit tuned into God's will in any area, there will be some things you just *think* of and, before you can confess it, it will show up. For example, I thought about a Rolex watch one day and, later that day, I walked into a room where a man there said to me, "You need to have a Rolex watch." And he gave me a Rolex watch!

"Well, I just can't see myself with a Rolex watch," you might say. That's because the devil has been holding back from you for so long. But I am aiming for him to turn everything loose that he has been holding back from you. *Everything!* Everything he has stolen from you—

everything he has held back from you all these years of your being blinded to the truth and steeped in religious tradition—he has to let it go! The stuff you should have had all those years, he has to turn loose! I dare you to say, "Devil, in Jesus' Name, I want my stuff now!"

I know what I'm talking about concerning commanding covenant wealth. This is firsthand experience that I'm speaking from. In First John 1:1 and 3, John said, *"That which was from the beginning, which we have heard, which we have seen with our eyes, which we have looked upon, and our hands have handled, of the Word of life.... That which we have seen and heard declare we unto you, that ye also may have fellowship with us...."*

I have "heard and seen" with my own eyes what I have shared with you in this book. My hands have handled covenant wealth. And I declare these things unto you. I don't have any need. I don't have any bills. I don't know how many millions of dollars my house cost, but it's paid for.

I'm telling you this to let you know that the "mystery" works today. And I'm not going to let any worldly folks— heathens or ungodly church members—stop me from testifying about what the Lord has done for me! Instead I give God praise that I am a covenant-walking, wealth-commanding money magnet for Him! Will you join me and allow God to do great things in your life too?

Prayer of Salvation

God loves you—no matter who you are, no matter what your past. God loves you so much that He gave His one and only begotten Son for you. The Bible tells us that "...whoever believes in him shall not perish but have eternal life" (John 3:16 *NIV*). Jesus laid down His life and rose again so that we could spend eternity with Him in Heaven and experience His absolute best on earth. If you would like to receive Jesus into your life, say the following prayer out loud and mean it from your heart.

> *Heavenly Father, I come to You admitting that I am a sinner. Right now, I choose to turn away from sin, and I ask You to cleanse me from all unrighteousness. I believe that Your Son Jesus died on the Cross to take away my sins. I also believe that He rose again from the dead so that I might be forgiven of my sins and made righteous through faith in Him. I call upon the Name of Jesus Christ to be the Savior and Lord of my life. Jesus, I choose to follow You and ask that You fill me with the power of the Holy Spirit. I declare that right now I am a child of God. I am free from sin and full of the righteousness of God. I am saved in Jesus' Name. Amen.*

If you prayed this prayer to receive Jesus Christ as your Savior for the first time, please write us to receive more information about your new life in Christ.

You may write to us at:
Ever Increasing Word Ministries
P.O. Box 7
Darrow, LA 70725

About the Author

Dr. Leroy Thompson Sr. is the pastor and founder of Word of Life Christian Center in Darrow, Louisiana, a growing and thriving body of believers from various walks of life. He has been in the ministry since 1973, serving as a pastor since 1976. Even though he completed his undergraduate degree and theology doctorate and was an instructor for several years at a Christian Bible college in Louisiana, it wasn't until 1983, when he received the baptism in the Holy Spirit, that the revelation knowledge of God's Word changed his life; and it continues to increase his ministry. Dr. Thompson attributes the success of his life and ministry to his reliance on the Word of God, being filled with the Holy Spirit, and being led by the Spirit of God. Today Dr. Thompson travels across the United States taking the message of ministerial excellence, dedication, and discipline to the Body of Christ.

To contact Dr. Leroy Thompson Sr., write:

Dr. Leroy Thompson Sr.
Ever Increasing Word Ministries
P.O. Box 7
Darrow, Louisiana 70725

*Please include your prayer requests
and comments when you write.*

Other Books by Dr. Leroy Thompson Sr.

Money Cometh to the Body of Christ!
You're Not Broke—You Have A Seed!
Money, Thou Art Loosed!
How to Find Your Wealthy Place
I'll Never Be Broke Another Day in My Life!
Money With a Mission
What To Do When Your Faith Is Challenged
The Voice of Jesus—Speaking God's Word With Authority
Framing Your World With the Word of God

Order these books and other products by
Dr. Leroy Thompson Sr. online at:
www.eiwm.org

The Ever Increasing Word Ministries Vision

Changing the Lives
of People With
the Word of God

AND

Equipping the
Body of Christ to
Evangelize the World